THE

Stanley Gibbons Philatelic Handbooks.

STAMP COLLECTING
AS A PASTIME

BY

EDWARD J. NANKIVELL

MEMBER OF THE INSTITUTE OF JOURNALISTS
MEMBER OF THE PHILATELIC SOCIETY OF LONDON

London

STANLEY GIBBONS, Ltd., 391, STRAND, W.C.

New York

167, BROADWAY

1902

Stamp Collecting as a Pastime

Edward J. Nankivell

PREFACE

Many people are at a loss to understand the fascination that surrounds the pursuit of stamp collecting. They are surprised at the clannishness of stamp collectors, and their lifelong devotion to their hobby. They are thunderstruck at the enormous prices paid for rare stamps, and at the fortunes that are spent and made in stamp collecting.

The following pages will afford a peep behind the scenes, and explain how it is that, after nearly half a century of existence, stamp collecting has never been more popular than it is to-day.

And perchance many a tired worker in search of a hobby may be persuaded that of all the relaxations that are open to him none is more attractive or more satisfying than stamp collecting.

Its literature is more abundant than that devoted to any other hobby. Its votaries are to be found in every city and town of the civilised world. Governments and statesmen recognise, unsolicited, the claims of stamp collecting—the power, the influence, and the wealth that it commands. From a mere schoolboy pastime it has steadily developed into an engrossing hobby for the leisured and the busy of all classes and all ranks of life, from the monarch on his throne to the errand boy in the merchant's office.

In the competition of modern life it is recognised that those who must work must also play. The physician assures us that the man who allows himself no relaxation, no recreation, loses his energy, and ages earlier than the man who judiciously alternates work and play.

As stamp collecting may be indulged in by all ages, and at all seasons, it is becoming more and more the favourite indoor relaxation with brain-workers. It may be taken up or laid down at any time, and at any stage. Its cost may be limited to shillings or pounds, and it may be made a pleasant pursuit or an engrossing study, or it may even be diverted into money-making purposes.

So absorbing is the hobby that in stamp circles there is a saying, "Once a stamp collector, always a stamp collector."

CONTENTS

I.

As a Pastime.

According to the authorities, the central idea of a pastime is "that it is so positively agreeable that it lets time slip by unnoticed; as, to turn work into pastime." And recreation is described as "that sort of play or agreeable occupation which refreshes the tired person, making him as good as new."

Stamp collectors may fairly claim that their hobby serves the double purpose of a pastime and a recreation. As a pastime, it certainly makes time pass most agreeably; for the true student of the postal issues of the world, it turns work into a pastime. As a recreation, it is of such an engrossing character that it may be relied upon to afford the pleasant diversion from business worries that so many tired mental workers need nowadays.

For nearly half a century it has maintained unbroken its hold as one of the most popular of all forms of relaxation, and its popularity extends to all classes and to all countries.

But this very devotion of stamp collectors to their hobby has puzzled and excited the uninitiated. The ordinary individual, especially the man who has no soul for a hobby of any kind, regards it as a passing fancy, a harmless craze, a fashion that must have its day and disappear, sooner or later. But the passing fancy has endured for nearly half a century, the harmless craze still serves its useful purpose, and the fashion has acquired such a permanence as to convince most people that it has come to stay.

Of all pastimes, and of all the forms of recreation, not one can claim more lifelong devotees than this same stamp collecting. And where is another pastime with such international ramifications? In every civilised country, in every city, and in every town of any importance, the wide world over, thoughtful men and women are to be found formed into sociable groups, or societies, quietly and pleasantly enjoying themselves in the harmless and enduring pursuit of stamp collecting.

There must be some reason for this popularity, this devotion of all classes to a pursuit, this unbroken record of progress. It cannot be satisfactorily accounted for as a passing fancy or fashion. It has too long stood the test of years to be so easily explained away. Fancies and fashions come and go, but stamp collecting flourishes from decade to decade. Princes and peers, merchants and members of Parliament, solicitors and barristers, schoolboys and octogenarians, all follow this postal Pied Piper of Hamelin,

> "Grave old plodders, gay young friskers, Fathers, mothers, uncles, cousins,"

all bent upon the pursuit of this pleasure-yielding hobby.

Why is it? Whence comes the fascination?

To the unprejudiced inquirer the reply is simple. To the leisured man it affords a stimulating occupation, with a spice of competition; to the busy professional man it yields the delight of a recreative change; to the studious, an inexhaustible scope for profitable research; to the old, the sociability of a pursuit popular with old and young alike; to the young, a hobby prolific of novelty, and one, moreover, that harmonises with school studies in historical and geographical directions; to the money maker, an opening for occasional speculation; and to all, a satisfying combination of a safe investment and a pleasure-yielding study.

Old postage stamps—bits of paper, as they are contemptuously called by some people—may have no intrinsic value, but they are, nevertheless, rich in memories of history and of art; they link the past with the present; they mark the march of empires and the federation of states, the rise and fall of dynasties, and the peaceful extension of postal communication between the peoples of the world; and, some day in the distant future, they may celebrate even yet more important victories of peace.

II.

The Charm of Stamp Collecting.

His Royal Highness the Prince of Wales, in a letter to a correspondent, referring to stamp collecting, wrote: "It is one of the greatest pleasures of my life"; and the testimony of the Prince of Wales is the testimony of thousands who have taken up this engrossing hobby.

The pursuit of a hobby is very often a question of expense. Many interesting lines of collecting are practically closed to all but the wealthy. But stamp collecting is open to all, for the expenditure may in its case be limited at the will of the collector to shillings or pounds. Indeed, the adaptability of this hobby is one of its chiefest charms. The rich collector may make his choice amongst the most expensive countries, whilst the man of moderate means will wisely confine himself to equally interesting countries whose stamps have not gone beyond the reach of the man who does not wish to make his hobby an expensive one. The schoolboy may get together a very respectable little collection by the judicious expenditure of small savings from his pocket money, and the millionaire will find ample scope for his surplus wealth in the fine range of varieties that gem the issues of many of the oldest stamp-issuing countries, and which only the fortunate few can hope to possess.

In all there are over three hundred countries from which to make a selection. In the early days collectors took all countries, but as country after country followed the lead of England in issuing adhesive stamps for the prepayment of postage, and as series followed series of new designs in each country, the task of covering the whole ground became more and more hopeless, and collector after collector began first to restrict his lines to continents, and then to groups or countries, till now only the wealthy and leisured few attempt to make a collection of the world's postal issues.

This necessary restriction of collecting to groups and individual countries has led to specialism. The specialist concentrates his attention upon the issues of a group or country, and he prosecutes the study of the stamps of his chosen country with all the thoroughness of the modern specialist. He unearths from forgotten State documents and dusty files of official gazettes the official announcements authorising each issue. He inquires into questions surrounding the choice of designs, the why and wherefore of the chosen design, the name of the engraver, the materials and processes used in the production of the plates, the size of the plates, and the varying qualities of the paper and ink used for printing the stamps— in fact, nothing that can complete the history of an issue, from its inception to its use by the public, escapes his attention. He constitutes himself, in truth, the historian of postal issues. The scope for interesting study thus opened up is almost boundless. It includes inquiries into questions of heraldry in designs, of currency in the denominations used, of methods of engraving dies, of the transference of the die to plates, of printing from steel plates and from lithographic stones, of the progress of those arts in various countries, of the manufacture, the variety, and the quality of the paper used—from the excellent hand-made papers of early days to the commonest printing papers of the present day—of postal revenues and postal developments, of the crude postal issues of earliest times, and the exquisite machine engraving of many current issues.

He who fails to see any justification for money spent and time given up to the collecting of postage stamps will scarcely deny that these lines of study, which by no means exhaust the list, can scarcely fail to be both fascinating and profitable, even when regarded from a purely educational standpoint. It is true it may be contended that all collectors do not go thus deeply into stamp collecting as a study; nevertheless the tendency sets so strongly in the direction of combining study with the pleasure of collecting, that the man who nowadays neglects to study his stamps is apt to fall markedly behind in the competition that is ever stimulating the stamp collector in his pleasant and friendly rivalry with his fellows.

Then, again, an ever-increasing supply of new issues from one or other of the many groups of stamp-issuing countries periodically revives the interest of the flagging collector, and binds him afresh to the hobby of his choice. Old, seasoned collectors, whose interest once set never flags from youth to age, relegate new issues to a back seat. They find more than enough to engage their lifelong devotion in the grand old issues of the early settlements. But the collector of modern issues who cannot afford to indulge in the great rarities, finds new issues a source of perpetual enjoyment. They follow one another month after month, and infuse into the collector's life the irresistible charm of novelty, and every now and again an emergency issue comes as a surprise. There is a scramble for possession, and a spice of speculation in the possibility, never absent from a makeshift and emergency issue, that the copies may be scarce, and may some day ripen into rarity.

III.

Its Permanence.

Ever since the collection of postage stamps was first started it has been sneered at as a passing craze, and it has been going to die a natural death for the past forty years. But it is not dead yet. Indeed, it is very much more alive than it has ever been. Still the sneerers sneer on, and the false prophets continue to prophesy its certain end.

To the unsympathetic, the ignoramus, the lethargic, the brainless, everything that savours of enthusiasm is a craze. The politician who throws himself heart and soul into a political contest is "off his head," is seized with a craze. The philanthropist who builds and endows hospitals and churches is "a crank," following a mere craze. The earnest student of social problems is "off the track," on a craze. The man who seeks relaxation by any change of employment is certain to be classed by some idiot as one who goes off on a craze. You cannot, in fact, step off the beaten track tramped by the common herd without exciting some remark, some sneer, perchance, at your singularity.

The most ignorant are the most positive that stamp collecting is only a passing fancy of which its votaries will tire, sooner or later; and yet for the last forty years, with a brief exception, due to an abnormal depression in trade, it has always been on the increase. Indeed, it has never in all those years been more popular with the cultured classes than it is to-day. The Philatelic Society of London has an unbroken record of regular meetings of its members extending over a quarter of a century. The literature devoted to stamp collecting is more abundant than that of any other hobby. Its votaries are to be found in every city and town of the habitable globe.

"All very fine," say our bogey men, our prophets of impending evil; "but blue china has gone to the wall, autographs are losing caste, old books and first editions are on the downgrade, pipes are relegated to the lumber-room, metallurgical cabinets are coated with dust, and even walking-sticks survive only at Sandringham!" Just so. We are all—Governments, people, and weather—going to the bad as fast as we can go, according to the croakers, the wiseacres, and the self-appointed prophets. Nevertheless, stamp collecting has survived the sneers and the evil prophecies of forty years, and so far as human foresight can penetrate the future, it seems likely to survive for many a generation yet.

And why not? In the busy, contentious bustle of the competition of the day, the brain, strained too often to its utmost tension, demands the relaxation of some absorbing, pleasure-yielding hobby. Those who have tried it attest the fact that few things more completely wean the attention, for the time being, from the vexations and worries of the day than the collection and arrangement of postage stamps. In fact, stamp collecting has an ever-recurring freshness all its own, a scope for research that is never likely to be exhausted, a literature varied and abundant, and a close and interesting relation to the history and progress of nations and peoples that insensibly widens the trend of human sympathies and human knowledge.

What more do we want of a hobby? We cannot ensure, even for the British Empire, an eternity of durability: nations decay and fashions change. Some day even stamp collecting may be superseded by a more engrossing hobby. The indications, however, are all in favour of its growing hold upon its universal public. The wealth invested in it is immense, its trading interests are prosperous and international, and no fear of changing fashion disturbs either dealer or collector.

IV.

Its Internationality.

Wherever you go you find the stamp collector in evidence. The hobby has its devotees in every civilised country. Its hold is, in fact, international. In Dresden there is a society with over two thousand members upon its books; in out-of-the-way countries like Finland there are ardent collectors and flourishing philatelic societies. The Prince of Siam has been an enthusiastic collector for many years, and even in Korea there are followers of the hobby. Australia numbers its collectors by the thousand, and many of its cities have their philatelic societies, all keen searchers for the much-prized rarities of the various States of the Commonwealth. In India, despite the difficulty of preserving stamps from injury by moisture, there are numbers of collectors; one of the best-known rajahs is collecting stamps for a museum, recently founded in his State, and the Parsees are keen dealers. There are collectors throughout South Africa, in Rhodesia, and even in Uganda. Wherever a postage stamp is issued there may be found a collector waiting for a copy for his album. In no part of the world can an issue of stamps be made that is not at once partially bought up for collectors. If any one of the Antarctic expeditions were to reach the goal of its ambition, and were to celebrate the event there and then by an issue of postage stamps, a collector would be certain to be in attendance, and would probably endeavour to buy up the whole issue on the spot. The United States teems with collectors, and they have their philatelic societies in the principal cities and their Annual Congress. From Texas to Niagara, and from New York to San Francisco, the millionaire and the more humble citizen vie with each other in friendly rivalry as stamp collectors.

Many countries are now making an Official Collection, and there is every probability that some day in the near future most Governments will keep a stamp collection of some sort for reference and exhibition. Under the rules of the Postal Union, every state that enters the Union is entitled to receive, for reference purposes, a copy of every stamp issued by each country in the Postal Union. Hence every Government receives valuable contributions, which should be utilised in the formation of a National or Official Collection. And some day stamp collectors will be numerous and influential enough to demand that such contributions shall not be buried in useless and forgotten heaps in official drawers, but shall be systematically arranged for public reference and general study.

Not a few countries are every year rescued from absolute bankruptcy by the generosity with which collectors buy up their postal issues; and many other countries would have to levy a very much heavier burden of taxation from their peoples if stamp collecting were to go out of fashion.

So widespread indeed is our hobby that a well-known collector might travel round the world and rely upon a cordial welcome at the hands of fellow-collectors at every stopping-place en route.

International jealousies are forgotten, and even the barriers of race, and creed, and politics, in the pleasant freemasonry of philatelic friendships.

V.

Its Geographical Interest.

few years ago many heads of colleges prohibited stamp collecting amongst their boys. They found they were carrying it too far, and were being made the easy prey of a certain class of rapacious dealers. Now the pendulum is swinging in a more rational direction, and many masters themselves having become enthusiastic collectors, judiciously encourage the boys under their care to collect and study stamps as interesting aids to their general studies. They watch over their collecting, and protect them from wasteful buying. In some schools the masters have given or arranged lectures on stamps and stamp collecting, and the boys have voted such entertainments as ranking next to a jolly holiday.

The up-to-date master, who can associate work and play, study and entertainment, is much more likely to register successes than the frigid dominie who will hear of nothing but a rigid attention to the tasks of the day. In the one case the lessons are presented in their most repellent form, in the other they are made part and parcel of each day's pleasant round of interesting study.

The genuine success of the Kindergarten system in captivating the little ones lies in its association of play with work. The same principle holds good even to a much later age. The more pleasant the task can be made, the more ready will be the obedience with which the task will be performed. The openings for the judicious and helpful admixture of study and entertainment are so few, that one wonders that such a helpful form of play as stamp collecting has not become more popular than it has in our colleges.

Take, for example, the study of geography, so important to the boys of a great commercial nation. The boy who collects stamps will readily separate the great colonising powers, and group and locate their separate colonies. How many other boys, even after they have passed through the last stage of their school life, could do this? Little-known countries and states are too often a puzzle to the ordinary schoolboy, which are familiar places to the stamp collecting youth. Ask the ordinary schoolboy in which continents are such places as Angola, Annam, Curaçao, Funchal, Holkar, Ivory Coast, Liberia, Nepaul, Reunion, St. Lucia, San Marino, Sarawak, Seychelles, Sirmoor, Somali Coast, Surinam, Tahiti, Tobago, or Tonga, and how many of all these places, so familiar to the young stamp collector, will he properly place? Not many; and the same question might probably be asked of many an adult with even less satisfaction.

The average series of used stamps are now so cheap that a lad may get together a fairly representative collection for what he ordinarily spends at the tuck shop. Some educationists have advocated the making and exhibiting of school collections of stamps as aids to study. Such collections would certainly be much more profitably studied than most of the maps and diagrams that nowadays cover the walls.

With few exceptions, every stamp has the name of the country, or colony, of its issue on its face; and most colonial stamps bear some family likeness to the stamps of the mother country. Our British colonial stamps are distinguished by their Queen's heads; the stamps of Portugal and its colonies by the portraits of the rulers of Portugal; those of Germany by the German currency; those of France mostly by French heraldic designs; those of Spain by the portraits of the kings and queens of Spain. So that the postage stamp is a key to much definite, valuable, and practical information.

VI.

Its Historical Finger Posts.

When considered from the historical point of view, postage stamps attain their highest level of educational value. They are finger posts to most of the great events that have made the history of nations during the last fifty years. Here are a few out of many examples which might be quoted.

The introduction of adhesive stamps for the prepayment of postage found France a Republic. A provisional government had just been established on the ruins of the monarchy which had been swept out of existence in the revolution of 1848. As a consequence, the first postage stamp issued by France, on New Year's Day of 1849, bore the head of Ceres, emblematic of Liberty. Three years later Louis Napoleon seized the post of power, and, as President of the Republic, his head figures on a stamp issued in 1851, under the inscription "REPUB. FRANC." Two years later the Empire was re-established, and the words "REPUB. FRANC." were changed to "EMPIRE FRANC." over the same head. In 1863 the customary laurel wreath, to indicate the first victories of the reign, won in the war with Austria, was added to the Emperor's head. In 1870 the Franco-German War resulted in the downfall of the monarchy, and the head of Liberty reappears on a series of postage stamps issued in Paris during its investment by the German army. The issue of the stamps of Alsace and Lorraine in 1870 marks the annexation of the conquered territory.

Italy in 1850 was a land of many petty states, each more or less a law unto itself, and each, in the fifties, issuing its own separate series of postage stamps. The stamps of the Pontifical States are made familiar by their typical design of a tiara and keys, and pompous King Bomba ordered the best engraver to be found to immortalise him in a portrait for a series of stamps. The other states had each its own heraldic design till the foundations of the Kingdom of Italy were laid, in 1859-60, by the union of the Lombardo-Venetian States, the Kingdom of the Two Sicilies, the Grand Duchy of Tuscany, the Duchies of Parma and Modena, the Romagna and the Roman (or Pontifical) States with Piedmont. The first issue of stamps of the newly formed kingdom bore a portrait of King Victor Emmanuel II. with profile turned to the right. In 1863, after the Kingdom of Sardinia had been merged in the Kingdom of Italy, a new series was issued for united Italy. The same king's portrait appears, but turned to the left. In 1879 King Humbert succeeded Victor Emmanuel, and his portrait appeared on an issue in the year of his accession. The assassination of King Humbert and the accession of his son as Victor Emmanuel III. are followed by the new portrait of the new king on the current series of the stamps of Italy.

The stamps of Germany tell a somewhat similar story. They mark the stages of gradual absorption into a confederation of states, and the ultimate creation of a German Empire. The postal issues of Baden ceased in 1871, when the Grand Duchy was incorporated in the Empire. Bavaria, though also incorporated, holds out in postal matters, and still issues its separate series. Bergedorf was in 1867 placed under the control of the free city of Hamburg, and thereupon ceased issuing stamps. Bremen, Brunswick, Hamburg, Lubeck, Mecklenburg-Strelitz, Oldenburg, Prussia, Saxony, and Schleswig-Holstein formed the North German Confederation, and closed their postal accounts with collectors in 1868. Hanover became a province of Prussia after the war of 1866, and thereupon ceased its separate issue of postage stamps; and Thurn and Taxis followed suit in 1867. In 1870 the North German Confederation was merged in the German Empire, which issued its first postage stamp with the Imperial eagle in 1872. But the Empire is not yet sufficiently united to place a portrait of the Emperor upon its Imperial postal series.

Indian postage stamps, overprinted with the initials "C.E.F.", for the China Expeditionary Force, *i.e.* the Indian troops sent to China in 1901 to relieve the besieged Embassies, mark an historical event of no small import.

The early provisional issues of Crete of 1898 indicate the joint interference of the Great Powers in its affairs, and the later issues, in 1900, bear the portrait of Prince George of Greece as High Commissioner of Crete.

The Confederate locals of America, issued, in 1861-3, by the postmasters of the Southern States when they were cut off by the war from the capital and its supplies of postage stamps, and each town was thrown upon its own resources, proclaim the period of the great American Civil War.

Collectors are all familiar with the long series of portraits of past Presidents of the United States, from Washington to Garfield.

The stamps of Don Carlos mark the Carlist rising in Spain in 1873.

But amongst the most interesting of all stamps that may be classed as historical finger posts, none equal in present-day interest the stamps of the Transvaal, for they tell of the struggle for supremacy in South Africa. In 1870 the Boers issued their first postage stamp, and a crude piece of workmanship it was, designed and engraved in Germany. Till 1877 they printed their supplies of postage stamps in their own crude way from the same crude plates. Then came the first British Occupation, when the remainders of the stamps of the first South African Republic were overprinted "V.R. TRANSVAAL," to indicate British government. Then, in 1878, the stamps of the Republic were replaced by our Queen's Head. In 1881 the country was given back to the Boers, when they in turn overprinted our Queen's Head series in Boer currency, to indicate the restoration of Boer domination. And now, finally, in 1900 we have the second British Occupation, and a second overprinting of South African Republic stamps "V.R.I.", to signalise once more, and finally, the supremacy of British rule in South Africa. The Mafeking stamps are also interesting souvenirs of

a gallant stand in the same historical struggle.

The war which Chili some years ago carried into Bolivia and Peru has been marked in a special manner upon the postage stamps of Chili. As in the case of our own troops in South Africa, so the Chilian troops in Bolivia and Peru were allowed to frank their letters home with the stamps of their own country. So also the Chilians further overprinted the stamps of Peru with the Chilian arms during their occupation of the conquered country in the years 1881-2. Chilian stamps used along the route of the conquering army, and postmarked with the names of the towns occupied, are much sought after by specialists. These postmarks include Arica, Callao, Iquique, Lima, Paita, Pisagua, Pisco, Tacna, Yca, etc.

And so the stamp collector may turn over the pages of his stamp album, and point to stamp after stamp that marks, for him, some development of art, some crisis in a country's progress, some struggle to be free, or some great upheaval amongst rival powers. In fact, every stamp issued by a country is, more or less, a page of its history.

VII.

Stamps with a History.

There are numbers of stamps that have an interesting history of their own. They mark some official experiment, some curious blunder or accident, some little conceit, some historical event, or some crude and early efforts at stamp production.

What is known as the V.R. Penny black, English stamp, is said to have been designed as an experiment in providing a special stamp for official use, its official character being denoted by the initials V.R. in the upper corners; but the proposal was dropped, and the V.R. Penny black was never issued. For a long time it was treasured up as a rarity by collectors, but now that its real claims to be regarded as an issued stamp have been finally settled, it is no longer included in our stamp catalogues. In the days of its popularity it fetched as much as £14 at auction. It is now relegated to the rank of an interesting souvenir of the experimental stage in the introduction of Penny Postage.

Of curious blunders, the Cape of Good Hope errors of colours are amongst the most notable. In 1861 the 1d. and 4d. triangular stamps, then current, were suddenly exhausted, and before a stock could be obtained from the printers in England, a temporary supply had to be provided locally. This was done by engraving imitations of the originals. Stereos were then taken, and made up into plates for printing. By an oversight a stereo of the penny value was dropped into the fourpenny plate and a fourpenny into the penny plate. Consequently, each sheet printed in the required red ink from the penny plate yielded a fourpenny wrongly printed in red instead of blue, its proper colour; and every sheet of the fourpenny likewise yielded a penny stamp printed in blue instead of red. These errors are highly prized by collectors, and are now extremely scarce, even poor specimens fetching from £50 to £60. At the time, copies were sold by dealers for a few shillings each. Similar errors are known in the stamps of other countries.

Now and again the sheets of a particular value have, by some extraordinary oversight, been printed and issued in the wrong colour. In 1869 copies of the 1s. of Western Australia were printed in bistre instead of in green, and a few years later the twopence was discovered in lilac instead of yellow. In 1863 a supply of shilling stamps was sent out to Barbados printed in blue instead of black; but this latter error was, according to Messrs. Hardy and Bacon, so promptly discovered, that it is doubtful if any of the wrong colour were issued for postal use. In 1896 the fastidiously careful firm of De la Rue and Co. printed off and despatched to Tobago a supply of 6,000 one shilling stamps in the colour of the sixpenny, *i.e.* in orange-brown instead of olive-yellow. Several are said to have been issued to the public before the error had been noticed. Indeed, the firm at home is credited with having first discovered the mistake, and is said to have telegraphed to the colony in time to prevent their issue in any quantity.

Another and much more common error in the early days of stamp production was the careless placing of one stamp on a plate upside down. Stamps so placed are termed *tête-bêche*. They have to be collected in pairs to show the error. The early stamps of France furnish many examples of this class of error. They are also to be found on the 6d. and 1s. values of the first design of the stamps of the Transvaal, on the early issues of Roumania, on some of the stamps of the Colombian Republic, and other countries.

Stamps requiring two separate printings—*i.e.* stamps printed in two colours—have given rise to many curious errors in printing. A sheet passed through the press upside down after one colour has been printed results in one portion of the design being inverted. In the 1869 issue of the stamps of the United States no less than three of the values had the central portions of their designs printed upside down. The 4d., blue, of the first issue of Western Australia is known with the Swan on its head. Even the recently issued Pan-American stamps, printed in the most watchful manner by the United States official Bureau of Engraving and Printing, are known with the central portions of the design inverted, and these errors, despite the most searching examination to which each sheet is several times subjected, escaped detection, and were sold to the public. When, however, it is remembered that stamps are now printed by the million, it will be wondered that so few mistakes escape into the hands of collectors.

As a bit of conceit, the issue of what is known as the Connell stamp is probably unequalled. In loyal Canada, in 1860, Mr. Charles Connell was Postmaster-General of the little colony of New Brunswick, which in those days had its own government and its own separate issue of stamps. A change of currency from "pence" to "cents" necessitated new postage stamps. It was decided to give the new issue as much variety as possible by having a separate design for each stamp. Two of the series presented the crowned portrait of the Queen, and one that of the Prince of Wales as a lad in Scotch dress. Connell, apparently ambitious to figure in the royal gallery, gave instructions to the engravers to place his own portrait upon the 5 cents stamp. His instructions were carried out, and in due time a supply of the 5 cents bearing his portrait was delivered. But before many were issued the news spread like wildfire that Connell had outraged the issue by placing his own portrait upon one of the stamps. Political opponents are said to have taken up the hue and cry. The matter was immediately brought before the higher authorities, and the unfortunate stamp was promptly suppressed. Half a million had been printed off and delivered for sale, but very few seem to have escaped the outcry that was raised against them, and to-day copies are extremely scarce. Poor Connell took the matter very much to heart, threw up his appointment, and forthwith retired into private life. But the portrait of the bluff mechanic type of countenance will be handed down from generation to generation in stamp catalogues and costly stamp collections long after the authorities that suppressed him are forgotten.

Some folks question the appearance of the Baden-Powell portrait upon the Mafeking stamps as a similar bit of conceit; but whatever may be said in criticism of Baden-Powell's stamp, most people will be inclined to accept it as a pleasant souvenir of an historic siege and a determined and gallant stand against great odds.

But of all the portraits that have appeared upon postal issues, none probably occasioned so much trouble and fuss as that of the notorious King Bomba of Sicily. The most eminent engraver of his day—Aloisio—was commissioned to prepare an exact likeness of His Sacred Majesty. After much ministerial tribulation the portrait was approved and engraved, and to this day it is regarded as a superb piece of work. A special cancelling stamp had to be designed and put into use which defaced only the border of the stamp and left the sacred portrait untouched. During the preliminaries necessary to the production of the sacred effigy the fate of ministers and officials hung in the balance. One official was actually marked for degradation for having submitted a disfigurement which turned out to be a carelessly printed, or rough, proof impression.

Numerous stamps have been designed, especially of late years, to represent some historical event in connection with the country of issue. The United States, in 1869, in the confined space of an unusually small stamp, endeavoured to represent the landing of Columbus, and in another stamp the Declaration of Independence. In a much more recent series, stamps of an exceptionally large size were adopted to give scope for a Columbus celebration set of historical paintings, including Columbus soliciting aid of Isabella, Columbus welcomed at Barcelona, Columbus restored to favour, Columbus presenting natives, Columbus announcing his discovery, the recall of Columbus, Isabella pledging her jewels, Columbus in chains, and Columbus describing his third voyage. Greece has given us a set of stamps illustrating the Olympian Games. But collectors look with considerable suspicion upon stamps of this showy class, for too many of them have been produced with the sole object of making a profit out of their sale to collectors, and not to meet any postal requirement.

Crude productions of peculiar interest belong more to the earlier stages of the introduction of postage stamps. Local attempts at engraving in some of our own early colonial settlements were of the crudest possible description, and yet they are, because of their very crudeness, far more interesting than the finished product supplied by firms at home, for the local effort truly represented the country of its issue in the art of stamp production. The amusingly crude attempts which the engravers of Victoria have made from time to time, during the last fifty years, to give us a passable portrait of Her late Majesty Queen Victoria, have no equal for variety. The stamps of the first South African Republic, made in Germany, are very appropriate in their roughness of design and execution. For oddity of appearance the palm must be awarded to those of Asiatic origin, such, for instance, as the stamps of Afghanistan, of Kashmir, and most of the local productions of the Native States of India, marking as they do their own independent attempts to work up to European methods of intercommunication.

VIII.

Great Rarities.

f the many stamps that are set apart, for one cause or another, from the ordinary run, as having a history of their own, those that by the common consent of collector and dealer are ranked as great rarities are the most fruitful source of astonishment to the non-collector. They are the gems of the most costly collections, the possession of the few, and the envy of the multitude. In a round dozen that will fetch over £100 apiece there are not more than one or two that can lay any claim to be considered works of art; indeed, they are mostly distinguished by their surpassing ugliness. Nevertheless, they are the gems that give tone and rank to the finest collections. Some of them are even priceless.

To the average man it is astonishing that anyone in his senses can be so foolish as to give £1,000 for an ugly little picture that has merely done duty as a postage stamp. He contends there can be no intrinsic value in such scraps of paper, and that settles the matter, in his opinion. But is it not so with precious stones and pearls? They are of value merely because they are the fashion. There is no intrinsic value in them. If they were not fashionable they would be of little or no value. Long-standing fashion, and fashion alone, has given them their value. So it is with stamps; fashion has given them their value, and every decade of continued popularity adds to that value as it has added to the value of precious stones and pearls. There is no sign that precious stones are likely to become worthless by the withdrawal of popular favour. Fashion changes from one stone to another without affecting the popularity of precious stones in general. So it is with stamps. Fashions change from one line of collecting to another without in the slightest degree affecting the stability or popularity of collecting as a whole. Precious stones and pearls minister to the pride of the individual, and stamps to his pleasure; and each has its own strong and unshakable hold upon the devotees of fashion and pleasure. There is a fluctuating market in the case of each of these favourites, but I venture to think that there is, and has been for the past forty years, a steadier rise in the value of stamps than in the value of precious stones.

British Guiana, 1856, 1 c.—In 1856 this colony was awaiting a supply of stamps from England, and pending its arrival two provisional stamps were issued, a 1 c. and a 4 c. These were set up from type in the office of the *Official Gazette*. A small illustration of a ship, used for heading the shipping advertisements in the daily papers, was utilised for the central portion of the design. Of the 1 c. value only one specimen is known to-day, and that is in the collection of M. Philipp la Renotiérè (Herr von Ferrary). Doubts have been expressed as to the genuineness of the copy, but Mr. Bacon, who has had an opportunity of inspecting it, says: "After a most careful inspection I have no hesitation whatever in pronouncing it a thoroughly genuine one cent specimen. The copy is a poor one, dark magenta in colour, and somewhat rubbed. It is initialled 'E. D. W.', and dated April 1st, the year not being distinct enough to be read."

This stamp may safely be placed at the head of great rarities. Of its value it is impossible to form any opinion. If a dealer had the disposal of the copy in question, he would probably want between £1,000 and £2,000 for it, with a decided preference for the larger sum.

Mauritius, "Post Office," 1d. and 2d.—The best known, the most quoted, and probably the most popular of all the great rarities is the "Post Office" Mauritius, so called because the words "Post Office" were inscribed on one side of the stamp instead of the words "Post Paid." There were two values, 1d. and 2d. They were designed and engraved by a local watchmaker, and were printed from single dies, and issued in 1847. The tedious process of printing numbers of stamps from single dies was soon abandoned, and only 500 copies of each value were struck. Of those 1,000 stamps only twenty-two copies are known to exist to-day. There are in the hands of leading collectors two copies of the 1d. unused, and three copies of the 2d. unused, twelve copies of the 1d. used, and five copies of the 2d. used. These rarities were only in use for a few days, and were mostly used in sending out invitations to a ball at Government House.

The value, according to condition, is from £800 upwards for each value, but unused they are of course worth a great deal more.

Hawaii, 1851, 2 cents, blue.—Like so many rare stamps, this first issue of Hawaii was designed and set up from type in a printer's office. About twelve copies are known to exist. The stamp was in use but a very short time, as the Post Office of Honolulu was burnt down, and the stock of stamps of this first issue was completely destroyed.

This 2 cents stamp is worth about £750.

British Guiana, 1850, 2 cents.—This is popularly known as the 2 cents circular Guiana, because of its shape. A notice in the local Official Gazette, dated February, 1851, announced that "by order of His Excellency the Governor, and upon the request of several of the merchants of Georgetown, it is proposed to establish a delivery of letters twice each day through the principal streets of this city." Certain gentlemen were named as having consented to receive letters for delivery at their respective stores, and it was further announced that "each letter must bear a stamp, for which 2 c. will be charged, or it will not be delivered, and when called for will be subject to the usual postage of 8 c." A supply of the required 2 c. stamps was provided by a locally type-set design enclosed in a ring. It is said that this delivery of letters was discontinued soon after it was started, hence rarity of the stamp.

Only eleven copies of this quaint postage stamp are known, and its market value is probably somewhere about £600.

Moldavia, 1858, 81 paras.—This rare stamp formed one of a set of four of the first postage stamps issued in Roumania. The values were 27 paras for single letters travelling, and not carried more than about seventy miles, 54 paras for double that distance, 81 paras for heavier letters, and 108 paras for registered letters, all within the limits of Moldavia. The 81 paras is the rarest of the series, as will be seen from the following inventory taken in February, 1859, of the then unsold stock: —

27 paras, printed 6,000, sold 3,675.

54 "   "   10,000 "   4,756.

81 "   "   2,000 "   693.

108 "   "   6,000 "   2,568.

All these stamps were printed by hand on coloured paper in sheets of thirty-two impressions in four rows of eight stamps. An unused copy of the 81 paras has fetched as much as £350.

United States, Millbury, 1847, 5 c.—In the United States the general adoption of postage stamps was preceded by what may be termed preliminary issues, of a more or less local character, and known as "Postmaster stamps." These "Postmaster stamps" were issued by various country postmasters by way of experiment. The Providence stamp is the commonest example. One of the rarest is the 5 c. stamp, with a portrait of Washington, issued by the postmaster of Millbury, in Massachusetts, in 1847. This stamp is said to be worth about £300. There are others reputed to be equally rare. Among the local stamps issued by various unofficial carriers and express agencies, there are many of which very few copies are known, and as they are practically all held by enthusiastic collectors, and never come into the market, there are no data as to their current value.

Cape of Good Hope, 1861. *Errors of Colour.*—In making up the plate of a provisional issue of triangular stamps, pending the arrival of supplies from England, a stereo of the 1d. got inserted by mistake in the 4d. plate, and a 4d. in the 1d. plate. Consequently each sheet of the 1d. contained a 4d. printed in red, the colour of the 1d., instead of blue. And the sheets of the 4d., in like manner, each contained a 1d, which, when the 4d. was printed in its proper colour of blue, was also printed in blue instead of red, the proper colour. These errors are very scarce, especially in an unused condition. The 1d., blue, is the rarer of the two, and is worth about £70 used; it is not known unused.

Tuscany, 1860, 3 lire.—In the early days of stamp production high values, such as we are now accustomed to get from most countries, were very rarely issued. For nearly thirty years Great Britain was content with a shilling stamp as its highest value. In 1860 the Provisional Government of Tuscany issued a stamp of 3 lire, for which there seems to have been very little use. It represented but two shillings and sixpence of English money, but it is nevertheless one of the great rarities to-day, especially in an unused condition. Used copies are worth about £65, and unused about £120.

Transvaal, 1878. *Error "Transvral."* —This error occurred once in each sheet of eighty of the 1d., red on blue, of the first British Occupation. It was evidently discovered before a second lot was required, as it does not recur in the next printing of 1d., red on orange. It is a very rare stamp. Used it is worth about £50, but unused it is one of the great rarities, and has changed hands at about £150.

Ceylon, 1859, 4d. and 8d., imperforate.—Several of the first issues of this colony, designed and engraved by Messrs. Perkins Bacon and Co., and issued in 1857-9, are esteemed as great rarities in an imperforate and unused condition. The 4d., 8d., 9d., 1s., and 2s. are the rarest. The 4d., so long ago as 1894, fetched £130 at auction. These stamps are amongst the few great rarities that may be entitled to rank as works of art, and every year they are more sought after and more difficult to get in fine condition.

IX.

The Romance of Stamp Collecting.

The story of the development of stamp collecting, and of the trade that has sprung up with it, is full of romance.

Our publishers' business, with its world-wide ramifications, was begun by young Gibbons putting a few sheets of stamps in his father's shop window. The father was a chemist, and it was intended that the lad should follow in his father's footsteps; but the stamps elbowed the drugs aside, and eventually yielded a fortune which enabled this pioneer of the stamp trade to retire and indulge his globe-trotting propensities to the full. He sold his business for £25,000, and, still in the prime of life, retired to a snug little villa on the banks of the Thames. The business was converted into a Limited Liability Company, and the Managing Director may be said to be a product of the original business, for it was a present of a guinea packet of Stanley Gibbons's stamps that first whetted his appetite for stamp collecting, and eventually for stamp dealing. Mr. Gibbons had for a great many years conducted his business from his private house. The new broom changed all that, and opened out in fine premises in the Strand, W.C., where the Company now occupy the whole of one house and the greater part of the adjoining premises. In every room busy hands are at work all the day long endeavouring to keep pace with a world-wide business which began with a few sheets in the corner of a chemist's shop window in the town of Plymouth.

And now, looking back on the humdrum days of the beginnings of the stamp trade, what opportunities do they not seem to have missed! Could they but have foreseen the present-day developments, a few unconsidered trifles, valued at a few pence in those days, put away in a bottom drawer, would to-day net a fortune. Young Gibbons, amongst his early purchases, bought from a couple of sailors at Plymouth for £5 a sackful of triangular Cape of Good Hope stamps, a large proportion being the rare so-called Woodblocks, with many of the Errors described in the list of great rarities in another chapter. Those Errors he disposed of at 2s. 6d. each. They are now worth from £60 to £75 each. And the ordinary Woodblocks, which were so plentifully represented in that sackful, are now catalogued at from 50s. to £9 apiece. Strange as it may seem, those were the common stamps of those days, and they are the rarities of to-day.

A well-known collection, full of rare stamps of the value of from £5 to £50, has been largely formed by the fortunate possessor out of stamps for which he paid 2s. per dozen just a little over twenty years ago.

A leading collector once conceived the idea of scouring the little-visited country towns of Spain for rare old Spanish stamps, and a most successful hunt he made of it. He secured most valuable and unsuspected hauls of unused and used blocks and pairs of rare Portuguese; but before returning home he decided to treat himself to a trip to Morocco, and during that ill-fated extension of his tour he lost nearly the whole of his patient garnerings of rare Spanish stamps, for during an inland trip some very unphilatelic Bedouins swooped down on his escort in the desert and carried off the whole of his baggage. He, being some distance ahead of his escort, escaped, and brought home only a few samples of the grand things he had found and lost.

In all forms of collecting the hunt for bargains adds zest to the game, and probably more so in stamps than in any other hobby, not even excepting old china; and, as in other lines of collecting, the bargain hunter must be equipped with the expert knowledge of the specialist if he would sweep into his net at bargain prices the unsuspected gems to be found now and again in the philatelic mart. Many a keen stamp collector turns his years of wide experience to good account as a bargain hunter, and at least one innocent amateur is credited with netting a revenue which would make many a flourishing merchant green with envy.

Many a match has probably been due to stamp collecting. Not long ago we were told of a young lady who wrote to an official in a distant colony for a few of the current stamps issued from his office. The stamps were forwarded and a correspondence ensued. There was eventually an exchange of photographs, and finally the official applied for leave, returned home, and married his stamp collecting correspondent.

Truly the scope of the stamp collector for pleasure, for profit, and for romance is as wide as the most imaginative could desire.

X.

Philatelic Societies and their Work.

Most of the great cities of Europe, the British Colonies, and the United States have their Philatelic Societies. They are associations of stamp collectors for the study of postage stamps, their history, engraving, and printing; the detection and prevention of forgeries and frauds; the preparation and publication of papers and works bearing upon postal issues; the display and exhibition of stamps, and the exchange of duplicates.

The premier society is the Philatelic Society of London, which was founded so long ago as 1869, and has as its acting President H.R.H. the Prince of Wales. For over thirty years, without a break, this Society has held regular meetings during the winter months. Its membership comprises most of the leading collectors in Great Britain and her Colonies and many of the best-known foreign collectors. On the membership roll are three princes, several earls, baronets, judges, barristers, medical men, officers in the Army and Navy, and many well-known merchants. This society has published costly works on the stamps of Great Britain, of the Australian Colonies, of the British Colonies of North America, of the West Indies, of India and Ceylon, and of Africa. It publishes an excellently-got-up monthly journal of its own, which now claims shelf-room in the philatelic library for ten stately annual volumes. It has held two very successful International Philatelic Exhibitions, one opened by the late Duke of Edinburgh and the other by the Prince of Wales, then Duke of York. At its fortnightly meetings, papers are read and discussed on various matters relating to the hobby. Other meetings are held for the friendly exchange of duplicates.

In the provinces, the principal societies are those of Manchester and Birmingham. The Birmingham Society possesses a collection of its own, which it keeps up to date, as a work of reference for its members. Several of the societies hold periodical exhibitions, in which members compete for medals, and in many other ways they lay themselves out to encourage and promote the collection of postage stamps as a popular pastime.

The names of the various societies and the addresses of the secretaries are published at the commencement of each winter season in Stanley Gibbons' *Monthly Journal*.

Apart from their pleasant sociability, these societies are of immense help to the collector, especially to the beginner. At each meeting papers are read and discussed, in which the most experienced collectors retail, for the benefit of the less experienced, the result of their latest researches, and eminent specialists display their splendid and carefully-arranged collections for the inspection, edification, and enjoyment of their fellow-members. This continual meeting and comparing of notes, this concentration of study upon the issues of a particular country, gradually ripens even the veriest tyro into an advanced and experienced collector.

Under such conditions difficulties are cleared up, and the way made plain for wise and safe collecting. In too many lines of collecting the specialist carefully guards his knowledge for his own ultimate personal profit. The Philatelist, on the other hand, is more frequently than not generously and candidly helpful to his less advanced fellow-collector, especially if he happens to be a fellow-member of the same philatelic society.

XI.

The Literature of Stamps.

Few hobbies, if any, can boast of such a varied and extensive literature as stamp collecting. Expensive works have been published on the postal issues of most countries. They have been published in English, French, German, Italian, Spanish, Dutch, Danish, and Swedish. Those published in English alone would make a library of some hundreds of volumes.

From its foundation, in 1869, the Philatelic Society of London has set itself the task of studying and writing up the postal history of Great Britain and her Colonies. Towards the accomplishment of this great task, it has already presented its members with splendid monographs on the Australian Colonies, the Colonies of North America, of the West Indies, of India and Ceylon, two volumes on the British Colonies of Africa, a separate monograph on Tasmania, and last, and most ambitious of all, a massive and comprehensive history of the postal issues of Great Britain. All these works are expensively illustrated with a profusion of full-page plates and other illustrations, and they represent years of patient toil, far-reaching investigation, and untiring research. The *History of the Adhesive Postage Stamps of Europe* has been written in two volumes by Mr. W. A. S. Westoby, and the same author, in collaboration with Judge

Philbrick, some twenty years ago published a work on *The Postal and Telegraph Stamps of Great Britain*. Messrs. W. J. Hardy and E. D. Bacon, in a work entitled *The Stamp Collector*, have sketched the general history of postage stamps. Other works too numerous to mention here have been written from time to time for the edification of the stamp collector, and the list is continually being increased by the addition of even more important works.

One of the most interesting and comprehensive series of philatelic works, still in course of publication, was commenced by Messrs. Stanley Gibbons, Ltd., in 1893, in the form of philatelic handbooks. These handbooks are written by leading philatelic authorities. Each important country, *i.e.* important from the stamp collector's point of view, has a separate volume devoted to it, and into each handy volume is condensed as much as may be necessary to guide the advanced collector in specialising the postal issues of the country which he favours. There have already been published:—*Portuguese India*, by Mr. Gilbert Harrison and Lieut. F. H. Napier, R.N.; *South Australia*, by Lieut. F. H. Napier and Mr. Gordon Smith; *St. Vincent*, by Lieut. F. H. Napier and Mr. E. D. Bacon; *Shanghai*, by Mr. W. B. Thornhill; *Barbados*, by Mr. E. D. Bacon and Lieut. F. H. Napier; *Reprints and their Characteristics*, by Mr. E.D. Bacon; and *Grenada*, by Mr. E. D. Bacon and Lieut. F. H. Napier.

For the instruction of the beginner, Major Evans, R.A., has compiled an excellent glossary of philatelic terms, under the title of *Stamps and Stamp Collecting*; and there is, further, *A Colour Dictionary*, by Mr. B. W. Warhurst, designed to simplify the recognition and determination of the colours and shades of stamps—a by no means unimportant matter when the value of a stamp depends upon its shade.

But the most popular of all the philatelic publications are, of course, the monthly periodicals. The first stamp journal is said to have been *The Monthly Intelligence*, published at Manchester in 1862. It had but a short life of ten numbers out of the twelve required to complete Vol. I. But other journals followed in rapid succession, with more or less success, from year to year, till in 1893 a list of the various ventures in this line totalled up to nearly a couple of hundred. *The Stamp*

Collectors' Magazine, started in 1863, may be said to survive in Alfred Smith and Son's *Monthly Circular; The Philatelic Record,* established in 1879, is now in its twenty-fourth yearly volume; Gibbons' *Monthly Journal* is in its twelfth yearly volume; and *The London Philatelist* is in its eleventh yearly volume; and all may be said to be going strong. How many ordinary periodicals can boast of equally robust lives? And yet some people are still to be found who speak in all seriousness of stamp collecting as only a passing craze.

Properly speaking, tradesmen's catalogues can scarcely be regarded as literature, and yet it would be very remiss on my part to close this chapter without a reference to the excellent catalogues with which stamp collectors are provided. What other hobby can boast of such comprehensive and detailed catalogues, giving the actual selling price of almost every item, and regularly revised and brought up to date from year to year? Messrs. Stanley Gibbons' Priced Catalogue is comprised in four volumes:—Part I., The British Empire, 244 pages; Part II., Foreign Countries, 458 pages; Part III., Local Postage Stamps, 122 pages; Part IV., Envelopes, Post Cards, and Wrappers, 317 pages; in all, 1,141 closely printed double-column pages of small type, with thousands of illustrations. This excellent catalogue is at once guide, philosopher, and friend to the stamp collector. Some people irreverently style it "the Philatelist's Bible." It does not profess to be anything more or less than a mere catalogue of goods for sale, but it is an open secret that it represents the combined work and the combined knowledge of the best Philatelists of the day, and that neither trouble nor expense is spared to include within its pages everything that a collector needs to know to enable him to gather his treasures together, and to arrange them in the best possible and most authoritative order.

Much the same story might be told of the literature of stamp collecting in other countries. In the United States, in France, and in Germany there are numbers of robust periodicals, some stretching back into the early days, and there are scores of volumes of philatelic lore, many of which find a well-deserved place on the shelves of English collectors.

As an indication of the value attached to philatelic literature, I may mention the fact that an English collector recently paid over £2,000 for a by no means complete collection of works relating to stamp collecting.

XII.

Stamps as Works of Art.

Some artists scout the idea of attempting anything that may be considered a work of art in the ridiculously limited space of a postage stamp. The restriction of a postage stamp when viewed alongside a canvas measuring several yards in length and height is probably hopeless enough. Nevertheless, many a stamp collector who is not devoid of art can find stamps which seem to him to be entitled to rank high even in the art world. In beauty of design, in the exquisite workmanship of the best modern steel engraving, aided by the most delicate machinery, and in unequalled printing, there are many gems within the very limited space of a postage stamp that excite and deserve, and not unfrequently win, the admiration of the most exacting critics. There are scores of little medallions, mostly on the postage stamps of foreign states, that surely would pass muster with an impartial judge of art. They are not the rarities of the stamp album. Some are even regarded as weeds in the philatelic garden. They are too often made to serve the revenue-producing necessities of the issuing state, and for that reason probably, more than for any other, they are made as attractive as modern art applied to stamp production can make them.

Great commercial countries, producing their postage stamps by hundreds of millions, are as contemptuous in their consideration of the art possibilities of a postage stamp as the cynical artist whose days and years are devoted to the disfigurement of wall space. This country has no cause to be proud of the designs or the printing of its postage stamps. The chief consideration seems to be a low contract price for the production of recognisable labels for the indication of the prepayment of postage. That is the commercial view. And yet there are some foolish people who believe that an artist who could design an effective and acceptable postage stamp for the British Empire would add materially to his own fame and to the art standard of the Empire itself.

Brother Jonathan across the sea is not unmindful of art in the production of his postage stamps, despite his commercial inclinations and training. From the first he has put his patriotism into his postage stamps. The portraits of the Presidents, from George Washington to Lincoln, and from Lincoln to McKinley, who have ruled, wisely and well, the destinies of the great Republic, Jonathan engraves in his best style, in his own official engraving establishment, and proudly places upon his postage stamps for the admiration of all good citizens and the edification and envy of the effete old countries beyond the seas.

We, with our richer memories and our stately galleries of great men who have ruled or governed or fought through the centuries, must be content with an Empire postage stamp that is little better, from an art point of view, than an ordinary beer label, and we must be content to be told that it is the penalty of success, of the dire necessity of long numbers, and of a needy Treasury that sorely hungers for still greater profits from the Post Office.

Meanwhile, small struggling states revel in beautiful stamps. The latest trend is in the direction of miniature portraiture. The Argentine Republic and Bolivia have in recent years issued some very fine examples in this direction. A very useful innovation is the addition of the name under the portrait. In this way thousands have been familiarised with the names and faces of men who before were almost unknown beyond their own country. Historic features, such as those of Columbus and Pizarro, have occasionally been added to the growingly interesting gallery of stamp portraits.

The recently issued New Zealand picture series, illustrating most effectively some of the choicest bits of colonial scenery, and some of the rarest birds of the colony, engraved by Messrs. Waterlow and Sons, afforded an interesting and successful experiment in an art direction. As a result it is said that a strong demand has been generated in other colonies for similarly beautiful and localised designs in preference to the stereotyped mediocrity supplied by the ordinary label process.

XIII.

Stamp Collecting as an Investment.

When a stamp collector is charged with being extravagant, with spending money lavishly and foolishly on a mere hobby, he may very justifiably reply that even his most extravagant spendings may be regarded as an investment.

The ordinary investor in, say, industrial securities is fairly content if he can, with a little risk, secure a steady six or seven per cent. If he launches out into more speculative shares, yielding higher rates of interest, he must be content to face a much greater risk of the capital invested. Now, the severest test of an investment is the yield of interest over a series of years covering periods of depression as well as periods of prosperity. The stamp collector who has used ordinary discretion in his purchases may confidently submit his investment to this test.

Some years ago, when I was writing in defence of stamp collecting as an investment, I received a very indignant letter from a collector who had made a large collection, complaining that he had then recently endeavoured to sell, but could get only a very small percentage of his outlay back, and that the very firms from whom he had bought most of his stamps scouted the idea of paying him anything like what they had cost him. He therefore ridiculed the idea that stamp collecting could be regarded as a safe investment, as in his case it had been a delusion and a snare. He was quite right, and it is still possible to make big collections—of, say, five thousand, ten thousand, and even larger—of stamps that are never likely to appreciate, and it is possible to buy those stamps at such a price that any attempt to realise even a small percentage of the original outlay must result in a woeful eye-opener.

Let me explain. In the stamp business, as in all other branches of commerce, there are wholesale and retail dealers. The wholesaler buys by the thousand stamps that are printed by the million. I refer, of course, to used stamps. In some cases the price paid per thousand is only a few pence for large quantities that run into millions. The wholesaler sells to the retail dealer at a small advance per thousand. Those stamps the ordinary dealer makes up into packets at a further profit, but still at a comparatively low price. Good copies he picks out for sale in sets and separately. Those have to be catalogued. Therefore, the catalogue price of common stamps bought and sold by the million eventually comes before the general collector at "one penny each," and the man who makes a collection of common stamps of the "one penny each" class can scarcely be expected to realise a fortune out of his stamp collecting. When he offers his gatherings of years to the self-same dealer, and asks, say, only the half of what he paid, he is astounded when the dealer has the audacity to tell him frankly, "I can buy most of those stamps at a few shillings per thousand, and you want an average of a halfpenny each for them!" "But," retorts the collector, "I paid you one penny each for them years ago, and now you won't give me half that amount. A pretty thing investing money in stamps!" The reply of the dealer will be, "My dear fellow, you have put your money into the wrong stamps. I bought, and can still buy, those stamps wholesale at a few shillings per thousand, some of them at a few pence per thousand; but I have to pay clerks for handling them and sorting them out, other assistants for cataloguing them, and the printers for printing the catalogue, so that in the end I cannot afford to sell them *separately* for less than about one penny each, but if you want a few thousand of any value I can sell them to you at a price enormously below what you ask for your collection." The collector's eyes are opened.

It is impossible to get away from the necessity of regarding stamps as an investment. Even the schoolboy cannot afford to put his shilling into stamps unless he can be fairly assured that he may get his money back at critical periods, which will crop up even in school life. Indeed, it may be said that there are few, if any, stamp collectors nowadays who do not put more money into stamps than they could afford to do if there were not some element of investment in view. In some instances large fortunes are actually invested in stamps, and I was only recently told of a collector who had taken his money out of a very profitable business and put it into stamps, and had netted very much larger profits than he ever realised in his regular business. But to do that sort of thing requires a profound knowledge of stamps and a ready command of a very large banking account.

Generally speaking, the best countries from an investment point of view are British Colonials, especially those of the small colonies that have small populations, and therefore very small printings of stamps. Obviously, countries that put stamps into circulation by the million can never be a very good investment, so far as their common values are concerned. Those who buy with a keen eye on the investment purpose, always buy unused copies of uncommon values. Unused are not likely to depreciate, and they may appreciate.

In fact, it may be safely said that, all round, the thing to do in stamps is to buy *unused* for investment. When stamps are printed by the million, *used* supplies will be available for no one knows how long; but in the case of unused, when a new issue is made, the obsolete stamp is on the road to an advance in value. It is true dealers stock large quantities of all stamps, but there are so many countries to be stocked now that no dealer can afford to hoard unused to any great extent, and even if he did, the dead capital would be an item which would compel him to advance the price of unused to protect himself from loss. Let us say a stamp becomes obsolete this year, and a dealer buys £100 worth. It would be a moderate estimate to place the earning power of stamps at 10 per cent. In seven years that £100 hoard would, reckoning compound interest, represent £200, or double face. Of course, no dealer would hoard up £100 worth of a common stamp, but from the day that it becomes obsolete it must be hoarded up by someone, and interest must be accruing on the investment which will have to be added to the value of the stamp, unless someone is to stand the loss. It will, therefore, be obvious that unused stamps must appreciate while used may remain stationary, for the simple reason that the limit of supply has been reached in one case but not in the other.

Taking almost haphazard a few stamps, most of which have been within the reach of all collectors during the last fifteen years, the following table will give some idea of the appreciation in prices which has been steadily going on in good stamps:—

	1875	1880	1886	1890	1893	1897	1902
	s. d.	s. d.	s. d.	s. d.	s. d.	s. d.	s. d.
Bremen, 1867, 5 sgr., green, unused	1 0	1 6	2 6	4 0	5 0	25 0	17 6
Bechuanaland, 1886, 1s., used.	—	—	—	2 6	2 6	6 6	30 0
" 1888-9, 4d., unused	—	—	—	1 0	2 0	2 0	3 0
British Guiana, 1860, 1 c, brown. perf., used	3 6	4 0	12 6	30 0	32 6	80 0	80 0
Cape of Good Hope, 1d., Δ unused	0 4	0 6	1 6	2 0	4 0	8 0	15 0
Cape of Good Hope, 1d., Δ Woodblock, used	2 6	3 6	15 0	25 0	45 0	90 0	95 0
Cyprus, 1880, 6d., unused	—	—	1 6	7 6	12 0	30 0	25 0
" " 1s., unused	—	—	2 6	10 0	15 0	40 0	55 0
Danish West Indies, 1872, 4 c., blue, unused.	0 6	0 6	1 6	3 6	5 0	17 6	25 0
Danish West Indies, 1873, 14 c., unused	1 0	1 0	2 6	3 6	5 6	24 0	32 0
Egypt, 1866, 5 piastres, unused	2 0	2 0	5 0	8 6	16 0	22 6	25 0
" " 10 "	2 6	1 6	6 0	12 0	20 0	26 0	27 6
Gambia, 4d., imperf., unused	0 8	0 8	2 6	5 0	6 0	20 0	32 0
Gibraltar, 1886, 1s.	—	—	1 9	3 6	7 6	70 0	75 0

Hayti, 1881, 20 c., *unused*	—	—	2 0	2 0	2 6	7 6	20 0
Hungary, 1871, 3 k., litho., *used*	0 2	0 2	1 6	3 6	6 6	30 0	40 0
Newfoundland, 1866, 5 c., brown, *used*.	1 0	2 6	3 6	7 6	12 6	28 0	25 0
New South Wales, 1d., Sydney Views, *used*.	2 6	4 0	17 6	30 0	35 0	40 0	40 0
Orange River Colony, 1877, 4 on 6d., *unused*	—	1 0	1 0	3 0	3 0	5 0	30 0
Tonga, 1892, 8d.	—	—	—	—	2 0	5 0	10 0
" " 1s.	—	—	—	—	3 0	4 0	15 0
Transvaal, 1878-9, 4d., *unused*	—	0 8	1 0	1 0	0 9	1 6	20 0
" " 1s. "	—	1 9	2 0	2 0	4 6	15 0	40 0
Trinidad, 1896, 10s.	—	—	—	—	—	14 0	70 0
Turks Islands, 1879, 1s., blue, *unused*	—	1 9	2 6	3 0	5 0	20 0	25 0
Zululand, 1888, 9d.	—	—	—	1 6	1 6	12 0	17 6

Of foolish investors there will always be a generous supply, who will ever be ready to offer themselves as evidence of the worthlessness of any and every form of investment, forgetful of the fact that the shoe is more often on the other foot. In stamps, as in every other class of investment, the foolish may buy what is worthless instead of what is valuable. There are stamps specially manufactured and issued to catch such flats, and they are easily hooked by the thousand every year, despite the continual warnings of experienced collectors.

But if we turn to the result of experienced collecting we find abundant evidence of the fact that the stamp collector may enjoy his stamps and, when the force of circumstances compels him to abandon them, he may retire without regret for having put so much money into a mere hobby.

Mr. W. Hughes Hughes, B.L., started his collection in 1859, and kept a strict account of all his expenditure on his hobby, and in 1896 he sold to our publishers for close on £3,000 what had cost him only £69.

In 1870 a stamp dealer in London, as a novelty and an advertisement, papered his shop windows, walls, and ceiling with unused Ionian Islands stamps, which were then a drug in the market. The same stamps would now readily sell at 10s. per set of three; in other words, the materials of that wall-paper would now be worth at least £5,000.

The late Mr. Pauwels, of Torquay, made a collection which cost him £360 up to 1871, when it was put on one side and left untouched until 1898. It was then purchased by our publishers for the sum of £4,000, and yielded them a very fair return on their investment.

In the International Philatelic Exhibition, held in the Galleries of the Royal Institute of Painters in Water Colours in Piccadilly, London, in 1897, one collector marked over each stamp of his exhibit the price which he had paid for it, and the market price of the day. The collection had been got together during the previous fifteen years, and had cost its owner £25 2s., while by the then latest catalogue value it totalled up to £368 1s. 3d.

Shrewd business men are those who frequently invest large sums in stamps. The amounts spent annually by some wealthy collectors range from £1,000 to £10,000. One well-known Parisian collector, whose life has been largely devoted to his philatelic treasures, and who employs two secretaries to look after his collection, has, it is estimated, spent at least £200,000 on his stamps since 1870.

If investment were the Alpha and Omega of stamp collecting, every collector of standing would bemoan lost opportunities. Many a great rarity of to-day could have been had for a few shillings a few years ago. The Cape errors were sold by Stanley Gibbons at 2s. 6d. each. The "Transvral" error was sold by the same generous firm at 4s., and others in similar proportion in the day of opportunity.

To-day it is the fashion to look back with regret on those lost opportunities, and to nurse the belief that such opportunities are never likely to return. But experience shows that in every decade of stamp collecting the common stamp of to-day may be the rarity of to-morrow. In many a series of stamps some one of the lot from some cause or another gets scarce, and the price appreciates from year to year till the original price paid for the stamp in pence is represented by pounds.

XIV.

What to Collect and How to Collect.

The questions, "What to collect?" and "How to collect?" are much more easily asked than answered. Each individual will differ in taste, in inclination, in method, in time at his disposal, and last, but not least, in the depth of his pocket. The most that can be done is to outline a general plan, founded upon general experience.

Collectors are divided into two classes—the general collector and the specialist. The general collector takes everything that comes in his way, and knows no limitations, no exclusions of this country or that. The specialist, on the other hand, confines his attention to the stamps of one or more particular groups or divisions, or even to one particular country.

The most experienced collectors, whether general or specialist, almost invariably advise the beginner to start as a general collector. As a beginner he will have no experience to guide him in the choice of a particular group or division; and until he has travelled over the ground as a general collector it will be difficult for him to make a choice which he may not have cause to regret. As a general collector he will gather together a general knowledge of stamps in all their peculiar varieties, which can scarcely fail to be immensely useful to him even should he subsequently drift into specialism. Indeed, it is an accepted truism that the man who starts as a general collector invariably makes the best specialist in the end.

Starting, then, as a general collector, the beginner purchases an album—for choice say the "Imperial," published by Stanley Gibbons, Ltd., which on one page has a printed and illustrated list of the stamps of a country, and on the opposite page ruled and numbered spaces for every stamp mentioned in the printed list. A catalogue, setting forth the prices at which stamps may be purchased, should also be obtained.

One of the very first questions to be settled at the start will be the choice that must be made between the collection of used and of unused. The general collector who wishes to collect economically should certainly start with what is cheapest; and as the common stamps are cheapest in the used condition, used should be selected. When a collector can afford to spend his money liberally, the best and safest, and cheapest in the long run, will be stamps unused and in the pink of condition. Such stamps generally turn out to be a safe and not unfrequently a splendid investment.

The beginner will find that he can fill up a large proportion of the spaces in his album with comparatively common stamps, and these are much more economically purchased in the form of cheap packets. The blanks that remain will then represent stamps worth searching for separately, and buying singly as good opportunities occur. Many may be obtained in exchanging duplicates with other collectors.

After some experience as a general collector, preferences will gradually materialise, and the utter hopelessness of making a thorough collection of the postal issues of the world will be apparent. At this stage the collector generally sells the bulk of his collection, reserving only a few countries to be followed up in future on specialist lines. The remedy and the change are drastic, and, like most drastic remedies, are much too sweeping. Wiser and keener Philatelists nowadays retain their general collections, so far as they have gone with them, and upon their basis give play to their specialist inclinations. That is to say, they single out a country, and work at that exclusively on specialist lines; and when they tire of that country, or exhaust it so far as their means allow, they have in their general collection the nucleus of another country with which to build up another specialist collection. On this plan a collector can always be working in sympathy and on the lines of the fashionable country of the day. He can take up and open out whatever country happens to be the vogue. In this way a neglected country every now and again comes to the front, and the nucleus of that country which may be found in the general collection may suddenly acquire an interest and a value never dreamt of. A recent case in point is that of the Orange Free State. Its stamps went a-begging for purchasers. Then trouble, and unrest, and war brought them into notice, and now the almost worthless have become valuable, and the pence have run into shillings, and the shillings into pounds.

For many persons, however, limitations and exclusions are necessary from the start. In their case a choice must be made, and the safest choice will be that of the British Colonies, or, if a still more restricted line must be drawn, one of the Continental groups of Colonies. A glance at a priced catalogue will be the best guide for selection. If it must be an economical selection, the catalogue will speak for itself. There is abundant choice in every direction. There are colonies with few and simple and inexpensive issues, and there are others that require ample means and patient research. But the cheapest countries, from an expenditure point of view, are foreign countries — such as Sweden, Norway, Denmark, German Empire, Italy, Chili, China, and so on.

XV.

Great Collections.

reat collections of postage stamps, like great collections of pictures, in these days acquire an international rank and reputation. The great stamp collections of to-day are in a few hands, and have been built up by lavish wealth and lavish industry. Wealth alone will not suffice to gather together a really great philatelic collection. There must be patient research, and there can be no research apart from that full knowledge which comes only to the industrious and painstaking Philatelist. The gem that is wanted to complete the finest page in the rich man's collection has not unfrequently to be personally sought for in the byways, the alleys, and lanes of stamp collecting; and despite the keenest search of the wealthy, it sometimes, after all, falls by grim mischance into the laboriously gathered collection of the man of very limited means.

The Prince of Wales is known to be an enthusiastic and keen stamp collector. He is the acting President of the Philatelic Society of London. During his recent tour round the world he displayed his great interest in the postal issues of the colonies which he visited, and brought home much valuable philatelic information and a number of proofs of sheets of old colonial stamps which will help to clear up many doubtful points. H.R.H. collects only the stamps of

Great Britain and her colonies, and he possesses many specimens that are absolutely unique.

The collection which was made by the late Mr. T. K. Tapling, M.P., is now in the keeping of the British Museum, having been bequeathed to the nation by its possessor, who was one of the most cultured and shrewdest collectors of his day. His collection was his life-work— from boyhood till his early death in 1891. It was largely made up of the amalgamation of great collections. In his day Tapling had the first pick in every direction, and, as a result, his collection is to-day one of the grandest and richest and most scientific general collections extant. Great rarities may be said to be conspicuous by their prominence and by their matchless condition.

But the greatest collection of all is that of M. Philipp la Renotiérè, of Paris, known to most collectors as Herr von Ferrary. In the course of the last thirty years he has purchased many well-known old collections, amongst which may be mentioned that of Judge Philbrick for £7,000, Sir Daniel Cooper's for £3,000, W. B. Thornhill's Australians, etc. M. la Renotiérè has been a large buyer in the leading capitals of Europe for a great many years. His expenditure with our own publishers is said to average from £3,000 to £4,000 a year. He employs two secretaries who are paid large salaries, one to look after the postage stamps and the other the post cards, envelopes, and wrappers.

Mr. F. Breitfuss, of St. Petersburg, who has been collecting since 1860, is credited with the third finest collection in the world. He is an omnivorous, but scientific general collector.

Mr. H. J. Duveen, the well-known art connoisseur of London and New York, although he did not take to stamp collecting till 1892, has already got together the finest collection, outside the British Museum, in this country. It is celebrated not only for the beauty of its specimens, but also for its completeness, neatness, and scientific arrangement. The value of the collection is probably close on £80,000. It is enclosed in seventy handsome Oriel albums.

Mr. W. B. Avery, head of the well-known firm of scale-makers of Birmingham, has one of the finest general collections. It is justly celebrated for the large number of great rarities that it contains, amongst which are the two rare "Post Office" Mauritius in superb unused condition. The collection cannot be worth at present far short of £50,000.

Mr. M. P. Castle, the Vice-President of the Philatelic Society of London, who succeeded the late Mr. Tapling in office, is one of the keenest of keen collectors. His general collection became so large that he parted with it in 1877, and then specialised in Australians. This latter collection he sold, in 1894, to our publishers for £10,000, at that time the largest sum ever paid for a single collection. He subsequently made a grand specialised collection of Europeans. This, arranged in sixty-seven volumes, he sold, in 1900, for nearly £30,000, and he has now returned to his love for Australians.

The Earl of Crawford and Balcarres is a collector of only recent date, but he has already formed a really magnificent collection based on broad historical lines. He confines himself mostly to the stamps of the British Empire, the United States, and the Italian States. His lordship is a member of the Council of the Philatelic Society of London, and, when in England, a regular attendant at its meetings.

The Earl of Kintore is also the possessor of a very fine collection of English Colonials, etc.; among his greater rarities being the "Post Office" Mauritius, the complete set of Hawaiian Islands (first issue), the 2 cents, rose, British Guiana, and many other gems. He also is a member of the London Philatelic Society.

In France the place of honour, after M. la Renotiéré, is deservedly taken by M. Paul Mirabaud, the well-known banker of Paris, whose magnificent collection of Switzerland was shown in the last Paris Exhibition. It forms, however, only a small portion of his fine collection.

In Italy probably the most famous collection is that of Prince Doria Pamphilj, which is exceptionally rich in the interesting issues of the Italian States.

In the United States of America there are many notable collections, several of them being worth from £30,000 to £50,000, amongst which may be mentioned the Crockers', of San Francisco, Mr. F. W. Ayer's, of Bangor, Maine, and Mr. Paul's, of Philadelphia.

In Germany the greatest collection is doubtless that of Mr. Martin Schrœder, the well known merchant of Leipzig.

Stanley Gibbons, Ltd.

CAPITAL, £75,000. ESTABLISHED 1856.

HIGHEST POSSIBLE AWARDS.

GOLD MEDAL, Paris, 1892.
GOLD MEDAL, Chicago, 1893.

FIVE MEDALS
(*Highest in each Class*),
GENEVA, 1896.

FOUR MEDALS
(*Highest in each Class*),
LONDON, 1897.

The above-mentioned high rewards gained by the Firm have been awarded for the perfect condition and completeness of Stamp Collections, and for general excellence in Stamp Albums, Catalogues, and Handbooks.

 Rare Stamps

Bought, Sold, or Exchanged.

STANLEY GIBBONS,

LIMITED,

New Announcements.

ANNUAL SALE OVER THIRTY THOUSAND PACKETS.

NOW READY, the following Popular Series of

PACKETS OF FOREIGN POSTAGE STAMPS

All the Stamps contained in the following Packets are warranted absolutely genuine, free from reprints. They are also in good condition and perfect.

These Packets cannot be sent by book post to Postal Union Countries. The cost by letter rate is 2-1/2d. for every 100 Stamps. The amount required for postage can therefore be reckoned, and should be added when remitting.

New and Improved Packets of Used and Unused Stamps.

No. 1.—The Sixpenny Packet of Mixed Continental Stamps contains 100, including many obsolete and rare. (This packet contains duplicates.) Post-free, 7d.

No. 2.—The Sixpenny Packet of Used Foreign Stamps contains 50 varieties, all different, including Egypt, Spain, Chili, New South Wales, Transvaal, Roumania, Porto Rico, Argentine, Sweden, Brazil, Turkey, &c. Post-free, 7d.

No. 3.—The Sixpenny Packet of Used Colonial Stamps contains 12 varieties, including Natal, Ceylon, India H.M.S., Cape of Good Hope, British Guiana, Mauritius, Tasmania, New South Wales Service, Victoria, Jamaica, South Australia O.S., &c. All different. Post-free, 7d.

No. 4.—The Shilling Packet of Used and Unused Foreign Stamps contains 50 varieties, including French Soudan, Spain, Bulgaria, Portugal, Sandwich Isles (head of King), Italy, Turkey, Finland, Brazil, Roumania, Portugal, Argentine Republic, Ecuador, Salvador, Greece, Mexico, Shanghai, Philippine Isles, Japan, and others rare. All different and warranted genuine. Post-free, 1/1.

No. 5.—The Shilling Packet of Colonial Stamps contains 25 varieties, including Cyprus, Natal, Jamaica, provisional South Australia, Victoria 1/2d. rose, surcharged Ceylon, Straits Settlements, India Service, Queensland, Hong Kong, Barbados, Swan River, South Australia, Centennial New South Wales, Mauritius, Malta, and others rare. All different and warranted genuine. Post-free, 1/1.

No. 6.—The Eighteenpenny Packet of Used Foreign Stamps contains 100 varieties, including Mauritius, Hong Kong, Finland, Japan 15 and 25 sen, Barbados, Chili, Brazil, Greece, Russia, Porto Rico, India envelope, Jamaica, Belgium, Spain, Canada, &c. All different and warranted genuine. Post-free, 1/7.

No. 7.—The Two Shilling Packet of Rare Used and Unused Foreign Stamps contains 100 varieties, including Porto Rico, Colombia, New Zealand, registered Canada, rare Turkish, Dutch Indies, Ceylon, Mozambique, Mauritius, Portugal, French Colonies, O. F. State, Cyprus, Norway, Sardinia, Belgium, West Australia, Chili, Egypt, Bavaria, and others rare. All different and warranted genuine. Post-free, 2/1.

Approval Sheets

and

Collections of Stamps.

NEW SHEETS OF STAMPS FOR BEGINNERS AND MEDIUM COLLECTORS.

We have just been arranging our Approval Sheets of Stamps on an entirely new and much simpler plan than formerly. The Stamps are mounted on Sheets, containing an average of 100 Stamps per Sheet. They are all arranged in the order of our New Catalogue. First, Great Britain and the Colonies, then all Foreign Countries. These Sheets contain about 5,000 different Stamps, and a Sheet of any particular country will be sent on demand. The Sheets arranged to date are over forty in number, and contain all Great Britain and the Colonies, and all Foreign Countries.

TO ADVANCED COLLECTORS.—For Collectors more advanced we have an assortment of many hundreds of small books of Choice picked Stamps of every Country or District in the World. Most of these special books contain twenty pages (5×3-1/2 inches), and can be sent by post in an ordinary registered envelope to all parts of the world. These books, as a rule, include Used and Unused Stamps, but Special Approval Books will be made up to suit individual requirements. Collectors writing for such should state if they wish for Used or Unused Stamps; if singles, pairs, or blocks of 4 are required; also, in Used Stamps, if special Postmarks are sought for. In all cases, in these books, we shall lay ourselves out to meet the special requirements of each individual client, whether the amount required be large or small.

Great Rarities are our Speciality. We have a large number of Stamps on hand from £100 to £750 each, and shall be pleased to give prices and particulars to advanced Philatelists.

We purchase really Rare Stamps at a much higher Cash Price than that paid by any other Stamp Merchant.

Grand Collection Packets.

NEW AND GREATLY REDUCED PRICES FOR 1902.

No. 64 CONTAINS 100 VARIETIES,

Including used and unused.

Price 6d.; post-free, 7d.

No. 65 CONTAINS 250 DIFFERENT VARIETIES,

Both used and unused Stamps, Envelopes □ and Post Cards □ and is well recommended as a capital start for a collector.

Price 3/-; post-free, 3/1.

No. 66, 500 VARIETIES,

And is strongly recommended as the cheapest collection of 500 different Stamps ever offered—the Stamps could not be bought separately for three times the marvellously low price at which it is now offered. The Stamps, &c., are clean, picked specimens fit for any collection. The best 500 varieties in the trade.

Price 6/-; post-free, 6/1.

No. 67, 1,000 VARIETIES.

This packet contains 1,000 different Stamps (and no Envelopes, Bands, and Cards), and is the cheapest packet ever offered by S. G., Ltd., satisfaction being absolutely guaranteed. The price it is offered at is the lowest ever quoted for such a collection, embracing as it does scores of scarce varieties, provisionals, new issues, and many very fine and obsolete varieties.

Price £1, post-free and registered.

No. 68, 1,500 VARIETIES.

Each specimen is in perfect condition, and the 1,500 different Stamps form a noble start for anyone. A large number of really rare and valuable Stamps are contained in this collection; but it is impossible to enumerate them, as we are constantly adding New Issues and Older Stamps when we purchase such. Satisfaction is guaranteed.

Price £2 10s., post-free and registered.

No. 69, 2,000 VARIETIES.

A grand packet for a dealer or collector, every Stamp being different and genuine, and thus forming a choice collection in itself or a stock to make up sheets or for exchange purposes.

Price £4 10s., post-free and registered.

No. 69A, 3,000 VARIETIES.

A very fine packet, containing many rare stamps, all arranged in order, and mounted ready to price or remove to a collection.

Price £11 10s., post-free and registered.

No. 69B, 4,000 VARIETIES.

A valuable collection, all mounted on sheets in order. Really good value; being sold by us to collectors at less than the price usually charged in the trade.

Price £18, post-free and registered.

Grand New Variety Packets.

In order to meet the wishes of a great number of our customers, we have prepared a series of packets, as under, entirely different from one another, no stamp in any one packet being in any of the rest of the series; and the purchaser of the series of eight packets will have 1,305 extra good varieties, and no duplicates.

These packets do NOT contain any Post Cards, cut Envelopes, Fiscals, or Reprints, and are well recommended as good value, and are only a small proportion of the Catalogue value of the single stamps contained in them.

No. 70	contains	500 Stamps of Europe, all different.		Price 7/6;	post-free,	7/8.
No. 71	"	125 Stamps of Asia	"	Price 7/6	"	7/7.
No. 72	"	125 Stamps of Africa	"	Price 7/6	"	7/7.
No. 73	"	105 Stamps of Australia	"	Price 7/6	"	7/7.
No. 74	"	125 Stamps of West Indies	"	Price 7/6	"	7/7.
No. 75	"	125 Stamps of South America, all different.		Price 7/6	"	7/7.
No. 76	"	100 Stamps of North America	"	Price 7/6	"	7/7.
No. 77	"	100 Stamps of Central America	"	Price 7/6	"	7/7.

The set of eight packets, containing 1,305 varieties, if all bought at one time, will be supplied at the special reduced price of 55/-. Postage abroad 2-1/2d. extra for each 125 stamps.

THE JUBILEE EXHIBITION PACKETS.

No. 78.—The "Queen's Portrait" Packet. 100 Stamps. Price 10s.

The Ten Shilling Packet contains 100 Unused Postage Stamps, each one bearing a likeness of HER MAJESTY QUEEN VICTORIA. This packet contains perfect specimens only, nearly all with original gum. This is a real bargain, but as an extra inducement to purchasers we present a specimen of a Diamond Jubilee Stamp with each packet; thus each buyer becomes a subscriber to H.R.H. the Prince of Wales' Hospital Fund.

No. 79.—The "Queen's Portrait" Packet. 100 Rare Colonials. Price £1 10s.

The Thirty Shilling Packet contains 100 rare unused Postage Stamps, each one bearing a likeness of HER MAJESTY QUEEN VICTORIA. The stamps in this packet are entirely different from those in No. 78, and purchasers of both will thus possess two hundred distinct varieties. Most of the English Colonies are represented by carefully-selected specimens of the higher value stamps. With this packet we present the Half-crown Diamond Jubilee Stamp; thus each purchaser subscribes that sum to H.R.H. the Prince of Wales' Hospital Fund.

No. 80.—The "Picturesque" Packet. 100 Pictures. Price 12s. 6d.

Contains 100 Unused Stamps in perfect condition, each one being especially selected for beauty, quaintness, or originality of design. Among others, we mention:

Natives Paddling on the Congo River.
Native Village and Scenery in the Congo District.
A Native Village in Djibouti. The Bridge of Sighs in Kewkiang.

ZOOLOGY IS REPRESENTED BY—The Elephant, the Hippopotamus, the Bird of Paradise, the Stag, the Codfish.

Three of the exquisite Portraits of Her Majesty, as depicted on the Canadian Jubilee Stamps, showing the Vignettes of the Queen in

1837 and 1897, form an appropriate addition to this choice and remarkable packet.

GREATER BRITAIN PACKETS

OF

British Colonial Stamps.

NO DUPLICATES.

Every Packet of this series contains different varieties, no Stamp being included in two Packets, and purchasers will by this novel method be saved the inconvenience of acquiring duplicates, which is as a rule the bane of most packet buying.

								Price	Post-free
								s. d.	s. d.
No.	111	contains	20	varieties	of	Stamps	of Asia	0 6	0 7
"	112	"	25	"	"	"	"	2 0	2 1
"	113	"	40	"	"	"	"	3 6	3 7
"	114	"	40	"	"	"	"	6 6	6 7
"	115	"	50	"	"	"	"	16 6	16 7
"	116	"	45	"	"	"	"	12 0	12 1
"	117	"	30	"	"	"	"	4 0	4 1
"	118	"	40	"	"	"	"	21 0	21 1
"	121	"	20	"	"	"	of AFRICA	0 6	0 7
"	122	"	25	"	"	"	"	2 6	2 7
"	141	"	20	"	"	"	of WEST INDIES	0 9	0 10
"	142	"	20	"	"	"	"	2 0	2 1
"	151	"	25	"	"	"	of AUSTRALASIA	0 6	0 7

" 152 " 30 " " " " 1 6 1 7

" 153 " 30 " " " " 4 6 4 7

FOREIGN COUNTRIES PACKETS

OF

European Stamps.

EVERY Packet in this series contains different varieties, no particular stamp being included in two Packets, and purchasers will by this method be saved the inconvenience of acquiring duplicates.

				Price.	Post-free.
				s. d.	s. d.
No. 201 contains	50 varieties of Stamps of Europe			0 9	0 10
" 202 "	40 " " " " "			1 0	1 1
" 203 "	50 " " " " "			2 0	2 1
" 204 "	30 " " " " "			2 6	2 7
" 205 "	50 " " " " "			3 6	3 7
" 206 "	60 " " " " "			7 6	7 7

THE 20th CENTURY PACKETS

Of Envelopes, Registered Envelopes, Wrappers, and Letter Sheets,

ALL UNUSED, ENTIRE, AND GUARANTEED GENUINE ORIGINALS.

NO DUPLICATES.

Every Packet of this series contains different Envelopes, etc., no piece being included in two Packets, and purchasers will by this novel method be saved the inconvenience of acquiring duplicates, which is as a rule the bane of most packet buying.

The prices of these new Packets are wonderfully cheap, as we are clearing off our stock of entires.

These Packets cannot be sent by book post abroad. The average rate abroad by letter post or parcel post varies so much that sufficient should be remitted, and balance, if any, will be credited or returned. The prices quoted "post-free" are for Great Britain only.

ENVELOPE PACKETS.

Section I. — GREAT BRITAIN & COLONIES.

No. 601.—Contains 29 common varieties, including Bechuanaland, Chamba, Cochin, Leeward Isles, etc. Price 2/-; post-free, 2/1.

No. 602.—Contains 36 scarce varieties, including Great Britain compound, Bahamas, Barbados, Canada, Cape, Ceylon, Gibraltar, Grenada, Heligoland, etc. Price 8/6; post-free, 8/7.

No. 603.—Contains 36 scarce varieties, including Newfoundland, New South Wales, St. Vincent, South Australia, Trinidad, and a really grand lot of Victorian. Price 10/-; post-free, 10/1.

No. 604.—Contains 47 varieties of Great Britain only, including a superb lot of the rarer compound Envelopes, old dates and high values; also scarce Registered Envelopes, Wrappers, etc. A very fine packet and good value. Price 40/-; post-free, 40/2.

No. 605.—Contains 50 *rare* varieties of Bahamas, Barbados, British Bechuanaland, British Central and East and South Africa, British Guiana, Canada, Cape, and Ceylon. Price 25/-; post-free, 25/3.

No. 606.—Contains 45 *rare* varieties, including some very scarce Ceylon registered, Cyprus, Gibraltar, Gold Coast, Grenada, Heligoland, and India. Price 27/6; post-free, 27/9.

No. 607.—Contains 34 varieties of the Indian States, including Chamba, Gwalior, Jhind, Nabha, Puttialla, Bamra, Charkhari, Cochin, Duttia, Holkar, Hyderabad, and Travancore. Price 10/-; post-free, 10/1.

No. 608.—Contains 29 scarce varieties of Leeward Isles, Malta, Mauritius, Newfoundland, New South Wales, New Zealand, and Niger Coast. Price 12/-; post-free, 12/2.

No. 609.—Contains 29 scarce varieties of Queensland, St. Lucia, St. Vincent, Sierra Leone, South Australia, Straits Settlements, Tasmania, Tobago, Trinidad, and Victoria. Price 12/6; post-free, 12/8.

SPECIAL OFFER.

Packets 601 to 609 inclusive, containing 335 different varieties of Envelopes, Wrappers, etc., of Great Britain and her Colonies. Price £6 10s. Postage extra.

ENVELOPES.

Section II.—FOREIGN COUNTRIES.

No. 610.—Contains 20 common varieties. Price 1/-; post-free, 1/1.

No. 611.—Contains 21 scarcer varieties. Price 2/6; post-free, 2/7.

No. 612.—Contains 21 varieties, including Argentine, Brazil, Ecuador, Guatemala, etc. Price 4/6; post-free, 4/7.

No. 613.—Contains 24 varieties, including Persia, Russia, Shanghai, Uruguay, etc. Price 6/6; post-free, 6/7.

No. 614.—Contains 41 scarce varieties of Argentine, Austria, Austrian Italy, Hungary, Belgium, Bolivia, Brazil, Chili, and Costa Rica. Price 16/6; post-free, 16/8.

No. 615.—Contains 62 varieties of Danish West Indies, Ecuador, Egypt, France, and Envelopes of *twenty* different French Colonies. Price 12/6; post-free, 12/8.

No. 616.—Contains 43 *rare* varieties of the German States, including very scarce Lubeck, Mecklenburg-Schwerin, Mecklenburg-Strelitz, Prussian, Saxony, Thurn and Taxis, Wurtemberg, etc. A really good packet and exceptional value. Price 50/-; post-free, 50/3.

No. 617.—Contains 40 varieties of Guatemala, Hawaiian Isles, Holland, Dutch Indies, and Honduras. Price 12/6; post-free, 12/8.

No. 618.—Contains 35 scarce varieties of Japan, including rare plate numbers, Liberia, Mexico, Monaco, and Montenegro. Price 20/-; post-free, 20/3.

No. 619.—Contains 30 varieties of Nicaragua, especially strong in the older issues. Price 6/-; post-free, 6/1.

No. 620.—Contains 38 scarce varieties of Paraguay, Persia, Peru, Portugal, Roumania, Russia, etc. Price 18/6; post-free, 18/9.

No. 621.—Contains 39 scarce varieties of Finland, Russian Local Envelopes, Shanghai, Transvaal, Norway, Sweden, Switzerland, Turkey, and Uruguay. Price 17/6; post-free, 17/9.

No. 622.—Contains 77 varieties of Salvador, including many really rare and provisional issues. A very fine and interesting set. Price 25/-; post-free, 25/3.

No. 623.—Contains 32 old varieties of the United States of America, including scarce dies and papers of the Reay and Plimpton issues, and the old 3 cent letter sheet on blue paper. Price 15/-; post-free, 15/3.

SPECIAL OFFER.

PACKETS 610 to 623 inclusive, containing 527 varieties of Envelopes, Wrappers, etc., of Foreign Countries. Price £9 5s. Postage extra.

THE 20th CENTURY PACKETS

Of Post Cards and Letter Cards.

ALL UNUSED, ENTIRE, AND GUARANTEED GENUINE ORIGINALS.

NO DUPLICATES.

POST CARD PACKETS.

Section I.—GREAT BRITAIN & COLONIES.

No. 650.—Contains 13 common varieties. Price 1/-; post-free, 1/1.

No. 651.—Contains 13 common varieties, different from the last. Price 1/-; post-free, 1/1.

No. 652.—Contains 16 common varieties, all different from those in the other packets. Price 1/3; post-free, 1/4.

No. 653.—Contains 24 scarce varieties of Cards, including Bangkok, Barbados, British Central Africa, etc. Price 4/6; post-free, 4/7.

No. 654.—Contains 26 scarce varieties, including Falkland, Gibraltar, Heligoland, Hong Kong, etc. Price 4/6; post-free, 4/7.

No. 655.—Contains 23 scarce varieties, including Nevis, Newfoundland, North Borneo, St. Lucia, St. Vincent, etc. Price 4/-; post-free, 4/1.

No. 656.—Contains 24 scarce varieties, including Tasmania, Tobago, Trinidad, Turks Islands, Virgin Isles, Zululand, etc. Price 4/-; post-free, 4/1.

No. 657.—Contains 38 rare varieties, including scarce Cards from Great Britain, Antigua, Bahamas, Barbados, Bermuda, etc. Price 10/-; post-free, 10/2.

No. 658.—Contains 47 rare varieties from British Central, East, and South Africa, Canada, Ceylon, Cape of Good Hope, Cyprus, Gambia, etc. Price 10/6; post-free, 10/8.

No. 659.—Contains 47 rare varieties from Gibraltar, Gold Coast, Grenada, Heligoland, Hong Kong, India, Chamba, Gwalior, Puttialla, etc. Price 12/6; post-free, 12/8.

No. 660.—Contains 39 rare varieties from Sirmoor, Cashmere, Jamaica, Labuan, Montserrat, Natal, Nevis, etc. Price 12/6; post-free, 12/8.

No. 661.—Contains 41 rare varieties, including New South Wales, New Zealand, Niger Coast, North Borneo, Queensland, St. Lucia, Seychelles, Sierra Leone, etc. Price 9/6; post-free, 9/8.

No. 662.—Contains 41 rare varieties from South Australia, Straits, Tasmania, Tobago, Trinidad, Turks Islands, Victoria, Western Australia, etc. Price 10/-; post-free, 10/2.

SPECIAL OFFER.

Packets 650 to 662 inclusive, containing a really grand collection of 392 varieties of Post Cards of Great Britain and Colonies. Price £4. Postage extra.

Section II.—FOREIGN COUNTRIES.

No. 670.—Contains 20 common varieties. Price 1/6; post-free, 1/7.

No. 671.—Contains 27 other common varieties. Price 2/6; post-free, 2/7.

No. 672.—Contains 38 varieties, including some scarce. Price 3/-; post-free, 3/1.

No. 673.—Contains 35 varieties, including some scarce ones. Price 3/6; post-free, 3/7.

No. 674.—Contains 31 scarcer varieties, including Austrian Italy, Hungary, Belgium, Congo, and Brazil. Price 6/-; post-free, 6/1.

No. 675.—Contains 31 scarce varieties, including Bulgaria, Chili, Colombia, Costa Rica, Ecuador, Morocco, Tunis, etc. Price 4/-; post-free, 4/1.

No. 676.—Contains 36 scarce varieties, including German East Africa, Greece, Guatemala, Hawaiian Islands, Holland, Curaçao, Dutch Indies, Surinam, etc. Price 6/-; post-free, 6/2.

No. 677.—Contains 45 scarce varieties, including Italy, Eritrea, San Marino, Japan, Luxemburg, Mexico, etc. Price 8/-; post-free, 8/2.

No. 678.—Contains 48 scarce varieties, including Monaco, Montenegro, Nicaragua, Orange Free State, Paraguay, Persia, Peru, Azores, Madeira, etc. Price 10/-; post-free, 10/2.

No. 679.—Contains 39 scarce varieties from Roumania, Russia, Finland, Servia, Shanghai, Siam, South African Republic, Spain, etc. Price 7/-; post-free, 7/2.

No. 680.—Contains 45 scarce varieties from Cuba, Norway, Sweden, Switzerland, Turkey, Uruguay, etc. Price 9/6; post-free, 9/8.

No. 681.—Contains 39 rare varieties from Argentine, Austrian Italy, Hungary, etc. Price 6/6; post-free, 6/7.

No. 682.—Contains 51 rare varieties from Belgium, Congo, Bolivia, Brazil, etc. Price 15/-; post-free, 15/2.

No. 683.—Contains 54 rare varieties from Bulgaria, Chili, Colombia, Costa Rica, Denmark, Iceland, etc. Price 10/-; post-free, 10/2.

No. 684.—Contains 54 rare varieties from Ecuador, Egypt, France, Tunis, Baden, Bavaria, etc. Price 10/-; post-free, 10/2.

No. 685.—Contains 72 rare varieties from Wurtemberg, Greece, Guatemala, Hawaiian Islands, Hayti, Holland and Colonies. Price 15/-; post-free, 15/3.

No. 686.—Contains 62 rare varieties from Italy, Japan, Luxemburg, Mexico, etc. Price 14/-; post-free, 14/3.

No. 687.—Contains 50 rare varieties from Monaco, Montenegro, Nicaragua, Paraguay, Persia, etc. Price 10/-; post-free, 10/2.

No. 688.—Contains 59 rare varieties from Peru, Portugal and Colonies, Roumania, etc. Price 15/-; post-free, 15/3.

No. 689.—Contains 78 rare varieties from Russia, Finland, Salvador, etc. Price 15/-; post-free, 15/3.

No. 690.—Contains 48 rare varieties from Shanghai, Siam, Spain and Colonies, Sweden, etc. Price 16/6; post-free, 16/8.

No. 691.—Contains 43 rare varieties from Switzerland, Turkey, United States, Uruguay, Venezuela, etc. Price 9/6; post-free, 9/8.

SPECIAL OFFER.

Packets 670 to 691 inclusive, containing a superb collection of 1,005 varieties of *Post Cards* of Foreign Countries; a bargain. Price £8 10s. Postage extra.

1/- each.

THE SEVENTH EDITION OF

The Improved Postage Stamp Album,

No. 0.

THE BEST AND LARGEST SHILLING ALBUM EVER PUBLISHED.

176 large pages. Spaces for 4,700 Stamps.

48 extra pages added in this Edition without extra charge.

This Album is now selling at the rate of over 1,000 copies a month.

The demand for this Album has simply been phenomenal, and it gives universal satisfaction—not a single complaint has been received. The last Edition had nearly 20 extra pages added, and now another 48 pages have been added, and all the Geographical and Historical Notes brought up fully to date. All the newest Stamp-issuing countries, such as Ichang, Las Bela, Tientsin, Bundi, Dhar, etc. etc., have been added. At the top of each page there is the name of the country, and a mass of valuable information, including date when Stamps were issued, population, area, reigning sovereign, capital, etc. Spaces of proper sizes are provided for all Stamps, and the book is bound in a superior manner in gilt cloth. The Album contains a pocket to hold duplicate Stamps, and fifty Stamps will be presented *gratis* with each Album. There is also an Illustrated

Frontispiece of the Rarest Stamps, with prices attached that we pay for each.

Price, bound in handsome gilt cloth, 1/-, or post-free 1/3.

E. S. says: "I asked a friend where the best place was to buy a Stamp Album cheap. He referred me to you, saying that he had bought one and sold it next day for 1/6, after keeping the stamps."

A. A. writes: "I received your Stamp Album on Thursday, and I wonder how you can sell it so cheap; for as soon as a friend saw it he offered me 2/- for it. Please send me another."

C. A. W. writes: "Please send me one of your marvellous 1/- Albums, with packet of stamps, in order that I may convince my incredulous friends that such a thing is possible."

Miss M. R. writes from Piccadilly: "I was greatly pleased with the Album I received this morning, which all my friends admired, and thought it very cheap."

THE
Improved Postage Stamp Album.

COVER OF NO. 3.

FOURTEENTH EDITION.

GREATLY ENLARGED AND RE-WRITTEN.

Size of Page, 10 by 7-3/4 ins.

One Hundred Stamps, all different, are presented with each Album sold.

This new Edition is printed on a *superior* quality paper, especially made for it. The shape is oblong, and spaces are provided according to the different requirements of the various countries.

A large number of guards have been provided so that the Album shall not bulge when full.

The Album is divided into Continents, and the name of the country only is given at the head of each page.

Fifty-seven different watermarks are illustrated in actual size, and lists are given of the various watermarks of the different countries.

Two pages of illustrations of *rare stamps* are given, with the price under each stamp that we will pay for it.

Special attention has been paid to the binding, which is exceptionally strong, and the covers are artistically designed.

PRICES (all well Packed).

No. 2.—Strongly and neatly bound in Plain Cloth, gilt lettered back and sides, 304 pages. Price 3/6; post-free, 3/11; abroad, 4/6.

No. 3.—Well bound in Art Vellum, as illustration, blocked in gold and colours, 304 pages. Price 5/-; post-free, 5/6; abroad, 6/2.

No. 4.—Handsomely half-bound, Art Vellum sides, gold lines and gilt letters on back, gilt edges, with extra leaves after each continent for new issues, making in, all 368 pages. Price 7/6; post-free, 8/-; abroad, 8/9.

EXTRA LEAVES

Can be supplied to this and the older small sizes, as under.

14th (New)
Edition.

Plain edges, for	Nos. 2 or 3	9d. per doz.;	5/- per 100.
Gilt "	" No. 4	1/3 "	8/6 "

12th or 13th
Edition
(smaller
size)

Plain edges, for	Nos. 2 or 3	6d. "	3/9 "
Gilt "	" No. 4	1/- "	7/- "

NEW EDITION.

☞100 POSTAGE STAMPS, all genuine and different, and of a catalogue value of over 8/-, are presented with each STRAND ALBUM.

THE STRAND POSTAGE STAMP ALBUM.

Well arranged, reliable, and thoroughly correct.

The book, which is printed on an unusually good quality paper, is bound in a new and specially designed cover. The shape is as illustrated, and the size a new and convenient one, viz. 9-1/2 in. by 7-1/2 inches. Sufficient guards have been inserted so that when the Album is full the covers shall be level with each other, and not bulged, as is often the case in imperfectly constructed books.

Nos. 15 and 16 include a series of Six Maps, specially engraved for this Publication, and beautifully printed in Colours.

No. 14.
320 pages. Spaces for 8,000 Stamps.

Nos. 15 and 16.
400 pages. Spaces for 11,000 Stamps.

Concise Geographical and other particulars with Illustrations are given at the head of each country, the pages being divided into rectangles, as is usual, with this most important innovation, that they vary in size so as to conveniently accommodate the Stamps desired to be placed in position. This is an advantageous improvement that will commend itself to every collector. Post Cards are not provided for, as all Philatelists of experience know it is best to collect them separately.

A new and very important departure has been made in Nos. 15 and 16, in including for the first time in any Philatelic Album a series of Six specially drawn Maps, printed in colours, and giving the names of all Stamp-issuing Countries. They are of course fully brought up to date, and are not needlessly encumbered with unnecessary names, so as to increase their usefulness for easy and instant reference.

Each Album now has four full-page Illustrations of the Watermarks found on all Stamps.

PRICES.

No. 14.—Strongly and neatly bound in plain cloth, gilt lettered, 320 pages, 2/6; post-free, 2/11; abroad, 3/4.

No. 15.—Strongly and handsomely bound in plain cloth, with gilt edges and lettering, and 6 Maps, and 80 extra leaves, 5/-; post-free, 5/5; abroad, 6/-.

No. 16.—Handsomely bound in half morocco, lettered on back, plain cloth sides, with 6 Maps, gilt edges, 400 pages, 8/6; post-free, 9/-; abroad, 9/6.

BLANK LEAVES. For No. 14.—9d. per dozen; 5/- per 100, post-free. For No. 15 or 16, gilt edges.—1/3 per dozen; 9/- per 100, post-free.

THE CENTURY ALBUM.

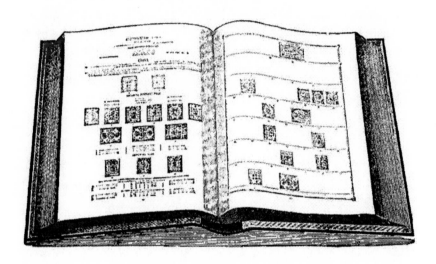

ALL THE WORLD IN ONE VOLUME.

NOW READY. In One Volume, 580 pages. Size of each page 10 by 13 inches.

The CENTURY ALBUM

OF THE

Postage Stamps of the World.

*Including a full Descriptive Catalogue, and Illustrated with several
thousand full-sized reproductions of the Stamps.*

This Album is produced in a very large edition at a cost of between
£2,000 and £3,000, and will be found to fulfil a long-felt want for an
Album in One Volume, of high-class style, and on thoroughly good
and highly surfaced paper, well and strongly bound.

The Century Album is printed on one side of the paper only,
catalogue and illustrations on the left, and numbered spaces to
correspond on the right-hand pages.

All minor varieties of perforation, watermark, and type are omitted, and only such varieties are included as can be distinguished by the young Philatelist.

Space has been provided for some 18,000 stamps, and provision made for new issues by the insertion of numerous blank pages.

IN TWO QUALITIES.

No. 21.—On extra stout highly glazed paper, strongly bound in cloth, gilt lettered and artistically designed cover, coloured edges.

Price 12/6; post-free in Great Britain, 13/4.

No. 22.—As last, but half bound in morocco, plain sides, raised bands, and gilt lettering on back, gilt edges; supplied in strong box.

Price 25/-; post-free in Great Britain, 26/-.

Extra Blank Leaves for this Album, 8d. per dozen, plain; or 1/- per dozen with gilt edges.

THE IMPERIAL ALBUM

(OPEN), SHOWING GENERAL ARRANGEMENTS.

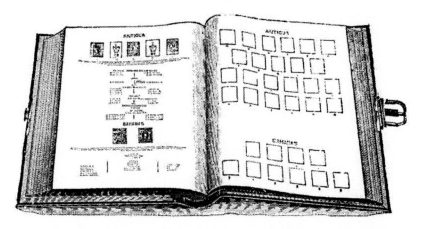

The Sale of these Albums averages over 6,500 per annum.

IMPERIAL ALBUM.

NOW READY. NINTH EDITION, 1902.

Great Britain and Colonies.

504 pages. Size of pages, 8-3/4 by 11-1/2 inches. About 1,800
Illustrations.

Since the publication of the previous edition of this Album, we have published the "Century" Album, designed for those who desire to collect in the simplest form, without regard to perforations or watermarks, and who desire a complete Album in one volume.

In order, however, to further the wishes of those who collect on more elaborate methods, the present edition has been prepared and very considerably enlarged, and for all practical purposes runs parallel with our current Postage Stamp Catalogue.

The close of the century marks an epoch in the history of postage stamps, and the present edition may be considered as

A PERMANENT ALBUM

Of the Postage Stamps issued during

THE NINETEENTH CENTURY.

New issues appearing after the date of this edition are best collated and arranged in blank albums, preferably with movable leaves, such as our ORIEL or PHILATELIC ALBUMS.

This Album is issued in FOUR qualities only (No. 6 has been discontinued) of paper, binding, &c.

No. 5.—On extra stout paper, bound in embossed cloth, gilt lettering, sprinkled edges. *Marone-colour covers.*

> Price without postage, 10/-; post-free in Great Britain, 11/-.

No. 7.—On extra stout paper, handsomely bound, extra gilt, bevelled boards, gilt edges, and patent expanding clasp. *Dark green covers.*

> Price without postage, 15/-; post-free in Great Britain, 16/-.

No. 8.—On highly rolled plate paper, extra strongly bound in half green morocco, lettered on back, cloth sides, gilt edges, no locks or clasps.

> Price without postage, 25/-; post-free in Great Britain, 26/-.

No. 9.—On highly rolled plate paper, magnificently bound in finest green Levant morocco, rounded corners, with gold line round the bevelled edges, lettered on back, gilt edges, patent expanding lock.

> Price without postage, 50/-; post-free in Great Britain, 51/-.

IMPERIAL ALBUM.

NOW READY. NINTH EDITION, 1902..

Foreign Countries.

870 pages, measuring 8-3/4 x 11-1/2 inches. About 2,400 Illustrations.

This Album is issued in FOUR qualities only of paper, binding, &c.
(No. 66 has been discontinued.)

No. 65.—On extra stout paper, bound in embossed cloth, gilt lettering, sprinkled edges. *Marone-colour covers.*

> Price without postage, 15/-; post-free in Great Britain, 16/-.

No. 67.—On extra stout paper, handsomely bound, extra gilt, bevelled boards, gilt edges, and patent expanding clasp. *Dark green covers.*

> Price without postage, 21/-; post-free in Great Britain, 22/-.

No. 68.—On highly rolled plate paper, extra strongly bound in half green morocco, lettered on back, cloth sides, gilt edges, no locks or clasps.

> Price without postage, 30/-; post-free in Great Britain, 31/-.

No. 69.—On highly rolled plate paper, magnificently bound in finest green Levant morocco, rounded corners, with gold line round the bevelled edges, lettered on back, gilt edges, patent expanding lock.

> Price without postage, 60/-; post-free in Great Britain, 61/-.

These Albums are too heavy for book post abroad, but can be sent by parcel post where same is in operation; the weight is about 8 to 10 lbs., and cost can be calculated for each country.

The PHILATELIC ALBUMS A to E.

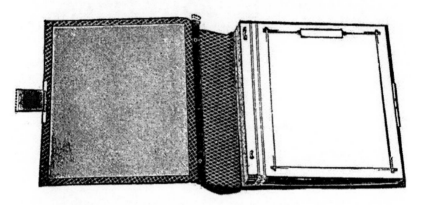

The "ORIEL" Albums are of a similar style, but more portable and in a superior binding.

The leaves in this Album are retained in their places by an original and newly patented plan, entirely doing away with the unsightly screws hitherto necessary on the outside of books of this class.

Pronounced by all who have seen it an ingenious and admirable arrangement, pre-eminently adapted for the purpose, and completely solving a difficulty experienced by collectors in general.

THE FIFTH EDITION OF

THE PHILATELIC ALBUM.

The most suitable Album published for Advanced Collectors.

Several important improvements have been introduced into this New Edition, suggested by increased experience, and greatly enhancing the use of this Work. Especially produced in answer to numerous inquiries for a really permanent blank Album. It will be found suitable for the reception of the most extensive and complete collection possible. It is also adaptable for Post Cards, Revenue Stamps, or entire Envelopes. Collectors using Albums of this class frequently resort to books not specially manufactured for the purpose, and hence unsuitable, or the more expensive and very often unsatisfactory mode of having them expressly made; it is to meet this want that this Album is published, and all that experience can suggest has been carried out to make it worthy the use of even the most advanced collectors, and adaptable to any arrangement that may be desirable.

It is likewise especially applicable for the use of those Philatelists who arrange their collections by the Catalogue published by ourselves or any other standard list. This Album is also peculiarly suitable for those who collect special countries only, taking as their guide the various lists published by the London Philatelic Society, etc. Each leaf has a double linen joint on an entirely new plan, allowing the leaves to set properly when the book is opened, and giving strength at the same time. A narrow marginal border embellishes each page, with a semi-visible network of quadrillé dotted lines, designed to assist the correct insertion of the specimens to be mounted. The leaves are 100 in number, and printed on one side only, on a very fine quality white card paper. They are movable, allowing rearrangement or extension into two or more volumes, as may be desired at any future time. It is hardly necessary to point out the advantage of this; moreover, if a page becomes spoilt, it can be at once replaced. A handsomely arranged title is included. An inspection is desired where possible.

PRICES.

A.—Strongly bound in half morocco, gilt ornaments and lettering; packed in a box, 30/-; carriage extra. Under 11 lbs., can be sent by parcel post for 31/-.

B.—Handsomely bound in full Persian morocco, bevelled boards, gilt edges, double-action expanding lock and key; packed in a box, 50/-; carriage paid, 51/-.

Spare blank linen-jointed leaves can be had, 1/9 per dozen, or 2/3 per dozen if with gilt edges, post-free; abroad extra. A sample leaf sent for 2-1/2d., post-free.

At the request of several London collectors we have prepared an Album of portable size, and convenient for taking to meetings of the Philatelic Society, etc. Our large blank Albums, as described above, are found to be too heavy and cumbersome for such purposes, and our new book will be found a very suitable one.

The size of the pages in E is 11 x 9-1/2. Weight, 7 lbs. 100 leaves.

E.—Strongly bound in half morocco, gilt ornaments and lettering; packed in a box, 25/-, or 25/9 by parcel post.

THE ORIEL

Postage Stamp Album.

This new album has been based on a special order from Mr. M. P. CASTLE, Vice-President of the Philatelic Society of London, to whom we have supplied 60 of these books, and to whom reference is kindly permitted. It has met with such an unusually favourable reception from those Collectors who have already used it that, on account of its general adaptability, it must undoubtedly quickly take a front rank in this class of publication. Amongst its numerous advantages, one especially may be named, and that is, its convenient size, rendering it extremely portable, and suitable for attending philatelic meetings, etc.

To those Philatelists who are unable to personally inspect same at our Establishment, a brief description will be acceptable:—

Each Album contains 50 leaves of the best hand-made paper, faced with Japanese tissue paper, so as to prevent all friction, and is bound in half red morocco, with cloth sides finished in gold. A space on the back of the cover is left plain, so that a Collector can have his books lettered or numbered to show the contents. Each Album is contained in a cloth drop-in case lined with lamb's wool. The leaves, unless specially ordered, are supplied perfectly blank, without any lined border or background, but if desired special leaves can be supplied with a fine quadrillé background, as supplied to the other Philatelic Albums of this form. Exact size of leaves from the outside edges, 10 inches by 10-1/4; available for mounting stamps, 8-3/4 inches by 10-1/4.

The price of the Album is 30/-; post-free, 30/7 (too heavy for post abroad, so will be sent carriage forward).

The Leaves, either plain or with quadrillé background, can be supplied at the price of 4/6 per dozen, or 32/6 per 100.

THE PHILATELIST'S COLLECTING BOOK.

FOR THE COAT POCKET.

With Patent Fastening to Flap.

Size, 6-1/2 by 4-1/4 inches. Handsomely bound in Art Cloth.

Each book contains 12 pages, having four strips of linen, 3/4-inch wide, arranged horizontally, glued at the bottom edge and with the upper one open, for the safe retention and preservation of recent purchases or duplicates. A large pocket is also provided at the back for Envelopes or Stamps in bulk. In daily use by leading London Collectors.

No. 17.—As illustrated. Price 2/6; post-free, 2/7.

No. 18.—Oblong, twenty-four pages, six strips on each page, interleaved with strong glazed paper to prevent rubbing. Price 5/-; post-free, 5/3.

THE MONTHLY JOURNAL.

Edited by MAJOR E. B. EVANS.

Published on the 1st of each month, and chiefly noted for:—

1st.—Verbatim Reports of all Law Cases of Interest to Philatelists.

2nd.—Earliest Information on New Issues.

3rd.—Largest Stamp Journal Published: recent numbers containing from 50 to 72 pages.

4th.—Quality of its Articles; with MAJOR EVANS as Editor this can be taken for granted.

5th.—Entirely Original Articles by the leading Philatelic Writers of the day.

SUBSCRIPTION—2/- per annum, or 5/- for three years.

Sample Copy sent gratis and post-free on application.

All Subscriptions must be prepaid, and commence with the JULY Number. The Prices for Back Numbers will be found in the current number of the *Journal*. There is no discount to the Trade.

The Monthly Journal now includes the Addenda to our Current Priced Catalogue. The old method of publishing addenda quarterly has been discontinued; and in the months of March, June, September, and December a Special Number of the Journal is sent to all Subscribers, containing lists of all Stamps, etc., that have appeared since the publication of the Catalogue. In the other months there will be quoted Special Bargains, Rarities, and prominent Alterations in Prices.

We therefore STRONGLY RECOMMEND *all purchasers of the Catalogue to* SUBSCRIBE TO "THE MONTHLY JOURNAL" —*forming, as it does, a complete continuation of the Catalogue up to date.*

The Stamp King.

A PHILATELIC NOVEL.

By Messrs. Beauregard and Gorsse.

Translated from the French by Edith C. Phillips.

The story commences at the New York Philatelic Club, and traces out in a most amusing manner the struggles of the two leading members to secure the rarest stamp in the world. The chase leads these collectors to London, Paris, and Naples, and ends, after many curious adventures, in New York.

EXTRACTS FROM REVIEWS.

The Daily News says: "A delightful addition to modern books of adventure.... Incidentally, there is a marvellous revelation of the inner affairs and methods of the stamp-collecting world; but the main interest of the book, to our mind, is its remarkable story, and it can and will be read with pleasure by many who care nothing whatever about the philatelic mania.... It would be spoiling a very good thing to tell the rest of the story of the adventures of these two, ... and we shall be much mistaken if this book, in popular form, does not meet with phenomenal favour."

The Spectator says: "A most diverting extravaganza, rather in the style of Jules Verne.... The apology of the translator for the lack of verisimilitude in the last scene is entirely unnecessary; otherwise she has done her work with credit, while M. Veilliemin's spirited illustrations heighten the attractions of a most entertaining and ingenious story."

The People: "A novel that will certainly interest the ordinary reader and doubly interest the Philatelist. It is profusely illustrated, and with a class of illustration that puts to shame much of the rubbish that we find in English novels."

The London Philatelist says: "It may at once be said that it is amusing in the extreme, and cannot fail to entertain all its readers. We have to heartily congratulate the translator upon the accuracy and excellence of her handiwork. *The Stamp King*, we should add, is both superbly illustrated and beautifully printed, and will assuredly command a wide circle of readers."

Vanity Fair: "This very sprightly novel on the stamp-collecting mania is most amusing, and might be just the thing for a present to young folks who are ardent collectors and readers of cheery, harmless fiction. It is excellently 'got up,' the illustrations are very good, and the story itself is quite exciting. All people who love (or loathe) stamp collecting are honestly advised to read the racy story of Miss Betty Scott."

The Liverpool Mercury: "The enthusiasm of Philatelists in their favourite pursuit is well illustrated in this capital story. It possesses many merits, the interest being sustained throughout. The translation is admirable, scarcely a trace is to be seen of French idiom, while the rendering into American vernacular is particularly clever and satisfactory."

The Court Circular: "A very great amount of interest is taken in stamp collecting, and a book pleasantly dealing with the stamp hobby, such as the one before us, will be sure to find a wide circle of readers."

The Lady's Pictorial: "This curious story is unique, for never before or since its publication has the stamp-collecting hobby been turned to account as the central idea of a really interesting romance and love story."

Gentlewoman: "The story is full of exciting incidents."

Half bound in Art Buckram, cloth sides, gilt lettering, plain edges, 200 pages, 80 fine illustrations. Price 6/-; post-free, 6/4; abroad, 6/8.

The Stamp Collector.

By HARDY and BACON.

This well-known and most interesting handbook was published in 1898 by Mr. George Redway in his *Collector Series*. On the failure of this publisher lately, we purchased the balance of the edition—about 1,200 copies—and are now able to offer the work at a great reduction on its original price.

The chief contents are as follows:

The Issue of Postage Stamps. Collecting—Its Origin and Development.—Stamps made for Collectors.—Art in Postage Stamps.—Stamps with Stories.—History in Postage Stamps.—Local Stamps.—The Stamp Market. —Post Cards.—Famous Collections.—List of Philatelic Societies.

Well bound in art cloth, gilt lettered, 247 illustrations, 294 pages.
Price 4/6; post-free, 4/10; abroad, 5/1.

The Mulready Envelope and its Caricatures.

This Work is a reprint in book-form, with a few alterations and additions, of a series of papers that have appeared in "The Monthly Journal." The book consists of 240 pages and some 45 full-page Illustrations of the most curious varieties of these interesting Caricatures. This New Work will be of interest, not only to Stamp Collectors, but also to those interested in Engravings—especially in the works of LEECH, MULREADY, CRUIKSHANK, DOYLE, PHIZ (H. K. BROWNE), THEO. HOOK, etc. etc. The Work has been produced in a very superior manner, and is printed on special paper with extra large margins; and by the kind permission of the Board of Inland Revenue an Illustration of the original Mulready is also included.

No. 1.—Strongly bound in extra cloth, gilt lettering, marbled burnished edges, &c., 6/-; post-free, 6/4; abroad, 6/8.

No. 2.—*Edition de Luxe*, handsomely bound, extra gilt, hand-made paper, with uncut edges, 10/-; post-free, 10/4; abroad, 10/8.

The "Philatelists' Vade Mecum."

(SECURED BY LETTERS PATENT.)

Is an entirely New and Original Invention for enabling Collectors to Mount Stamps without handling them, and is a *multum in parvo* of Philatelic requisites.

It consists of a pair of broad-headed flat metal tongs, one of which is fitted with a solid wedge. The object of this is to permit the free end of a mount held by the tong to be bent over, moistened, applied to the back of the stamp, and pressed down, and the mount can then be released, the stamp lifted, the other end of the mount moistened, and the stamp fastened thereby on the page. In the handle is inserted a glass of high magnifying power. On one side of the middle part is a millimètre scale (divided to half millimètres), and on the other a two-inch scale (divided to sixteenths), both accurately marked off. The stamp can be firmly held along either scale by the tongs. The tongs are made of solid nickel, polished, and fit into a handsome velvet-lined case, the size of which, when closed, is slightly less than 6 inches long, 1-3/4 inches wide, and only 1/2 inch thick.

PRICE, with case complete, 2/6; post-free, 2/7; abroad, 3/9.

SECOND EDITION.

REVISED TO DATE.

A GLOSSARY FOR PHILATELISTS,

ENTITLED

Stamps and Stamp Collecting.

BY MAJOR E. B. EVANS.

This Work is intended to fill a void which has hitherto existed in the Philatelist's Library. It will be found invaluable as a most useful and indeed a standard book to refer to in all cases of doubt or obscurity appertaining to Postage Stamps and their surroundings.

The Collector is not infrequently perplexed by the various terms employed, and the fullest explanations are here given of such.

Much interesting information is also included as to the various classes of and the manufacture of the paper employed, the typography, the embossing, the perforating or rouletting, together with many instructive and interesting details connected with the fascinating science of Stamp collecting.

Price 2/- in strong Paper Cover, 4/- in Gilt Cloth; post-free, 3d. extra.

A COLOUR DICTIONARY,

GIVING OVER

Two Hundred Names of Colours used in Printing, &c.

Specially prepared for Stamp Collectors by B. W. WARHURST.

Useful for many businesses in which coloured articles are bought and sold, and to give a more definite idea of the colours represented by certain names in common use, which are very frequently misunderstood.

SUITABLE FOR USE IN SCHOOLS.

Printed in TEN differently coloured inks on as many different papers, and further explained by diagram and ILLUSTRATED IN FIFTY-EIGHT COLOURS.

Price 2/6 in strong Paper Cover, 4/6 in Gilt Cloth; postage 3d. extra.

POCKET MAGNIFYING GLASSES.

After examining some scores of different sorts, we have been able to get one combining the greatest power with the largest field obtainable for pocket use. These glasses are mounted in handsome vulcanite frames, and are very compact. There are two lenses in each, which may be used singly, or if a very strong power is desired, may be combined.

Price 7/6; post-free, 7/7; abroad, 8/4.

SURCHARGE MEASURER.

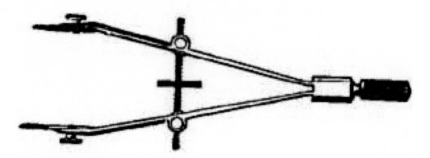

The accompanying illustration will give the best idea of what this is. It consists of a pair of needle-pointed spring compasses, capable, by means of an adjusting screw, of measuring with the greatest accuracy all surcharges up to 40 millimètres in length. In addition to the measure a millimètre gauge is obtained by running the head of the screw along a piece of paper, a series of lines exactly a millimètre apart being thus indented in the paper. For measuring surcharges on such stamps as Natal, Straits Settlements, &c., this will be found invaluable, and also in the detection of forgeries—a forgery or forged surcharge very seldom being *exactly* the same size as the original.

Price 7/6; post-free, 7/7; abroad, 7/11.

Prepared Stamp Mounts.

ACTUAL SIZE AND SHAPE.

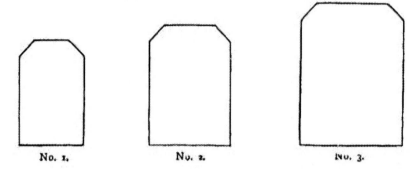

No. 1.   No. 2.   No. 3.

For affixing Stamps in Collections neatly and expeditiously. Far superior to the old plan of gumming the Stamps, and inserting them so that it is only with great difficulty they can be withdrawn. These Mounts are made of a thin strong white paper, and are ready gummed. By their use, Stamps can be removed at any time without injuring them, or in any way disfiguring the Collection. They are invaluable to those who collect watermarks. They should be used on the hinge system; thus, Moisten the Stamp, attaching the back of it to one half of the mount, the other half being fastened to the Album. The Stamp will then be facing the page; but do not turn it over until perfectly dry. A Collection with the Stamps mounted in this manner is far more valuable, if at any time a sale is desired. Three sizes are kept in stock: No. 2, medium size, suitable for ordinary-sized adhesives; No. 1, smaller size; No. 3, large size—for such Stamps as old Portuguese, or for cut Envelopes. This size may also be used for Cards by using two mounts for each card.

PRICES:

No. 1, 2, or 3 size, 3d. per 100; 1/6 per 1,000, post-free; 5,000, 6/6; 10,000, 12/-.

*The Prepared Paper can be supplied in Large Sheets, ready Gummed, at 3d.
per Sheet, post-free.*

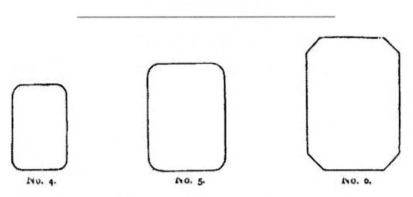

No. 4.　　　　　　　No. 5.　　　　　　　No. 6.

NEW CHEAP MOUNTS. At the request of many clients we have
prepared a New Cheap Mount, made from a thicker paper; a gum is
employed that permits the Mount to be removed from a book or
sheet without damage to the paper, or tearing the Mount, which can
thus be used several times over, such Mounts being particularly
serviceable for exchange clubs, or for use in dealers' stock books, &c.
The Mounts are put up in neat glazed card boxes, 1,000 of a size in a
box, and are sold in sets of three sizes, viz., three boxes and 3,000
Mounts for 2/6; 9,000, price 6/6; or *separately, any size,* at 1/- per 1,000
post-free

NEW SPECIALITY.

FOR STAMP COLLECTORS.

SPECIAL POCKET BOOKS, PURSES,

AND

CARD CASES.

Each of the following New and Useful Specialities has separate compartments provided for Postage Stamps, consisting of strips of thin celluloid protecting the stamps, and enabling them to be seen at once, and arranged so that the stamps can be put in or withdrawn in an instant without damage.

s. d.

70.—TUCK CASE FOR THE WAISTCOAT. Pocket size. 3-1/2 × 2-3/8. Very thin, made in morocco leather, lined leather of a neutral colour, with transparent pockets through which stamps can be seen.

Price 2/6; post-free, 2 7

71.—BEST MOROCCO GENTLEMAN'S CARD CASE, with usual pockets for visiting cards, and special compartments for stamps secured by a tuck flap fastening. (HIGHLY RECOMMENDED.)

Price 4/6; post-free, 4 7

72.—BEST MOROCCO WALLET. 5-3/4 × 3-1/2 inches. Lined leather throughout, flap and nickel lock fastening, gusset and tight pockets for letters; special provision for stamps under transparent pockets secured by an inner flap, and tuck fastening; leather covered notebook. (Highly Recommended.)

Price 10/-; post-free, 10 2

73.—LIMP MOROCCO LETTER CASE. Size, 6-1/4 × 4 inches. With gusset pocket for private letters, tight pocket for foreign post cards, and an array of transparent pockets for stamps.

Price 3/6; post-free, 3 7

74.—Ditto, ditto, with a gilt-edged ruled book under an elastic.

Price 4/-; post-free, 4 1

75.—BEST MOROCCO LETTER CASE, lined leather throughout, with gusset pocket for private letters, and special pocket containing an ingenious receptacle to hold a large assortment of stamps. Being detachable, it can be used either with or without the outer case.

Price 5/6; post-free, 5 8

76.—BEST MOROCCO PURSE. 4 × 2-1/2 inches. Flap and nickel lock fastening, stitched expanding pockets. The front to open out, displaying transparent pocket for stamps, with a separate flap to fasten. The purse can be used independently of the stamp compartment.

Price 6/6; post-free, 6 7

STANLEY GIBBONS'

New Stamp Catalogue.

5,000 NEW AND ENLARGED ILLUSTRATIONS.

POCKET SIZE, IN TWO VOLUMES.

VOL. I. contains all

ADHESIVE STAMPS OF GREAT BRITAIN AND THE BRITISH COLONIES.

New and Enlarged Edition. Price 2/-; post-free, 2/3.

VOL. II. contains the

POSTAGE STAMPS OF THE REST OF THE WORLD.

Price 2/-; post-free, 2/3.

Orange River Colony, Transvaal, and Mafeking Siege Stamps are transferred to Part I., being now English Colonies.

Particular attention has—in both volumes—been given to the production of enlarged illustrations of many minor varieties, which can easily be distinguished from a large print, but which are difficult to describe.

Many important countries have been thoroughly revised and re-written. *One hundred extra pages* have been added to the two volumes without any extra charge.

REAL MARKET PRICES.

It is, above all things, highly important that Collectors and Dealers should know the exact and real market values of all Stamps. This Firm has taken the greatest pains to arrive at these prices, and the prices quoted in these Catalogues are those at which STANLEY GIBBONS will supply the Stamps if unsold at the time of the order.

To facilitate business in all parts of the world, an Introduction, Details as to Approval Selections, Glossaries of Philatelic Terms, etc., are given in English, French, German, Spanish, and Portuguese.

STANLEY GIBBONS, LTD., 391, STRAND, LONDON, W.C.